BASIC
READING
POWER

BASIC READING POWER

Pleasure Reading • Comprehension Skills
Vocabulary Building • Thinking Skills

Beatrice S. Mikulecky / Linda Jeffries

LONGMAN

Acknowledgments

Our thanks to the many people who gave us valuable feedback on *Basic Reading Power:* Elizabeth Schmid, Orlando, Fla., Charlotte Seeley, Newton, Mass., and Sandra Sklarew, Reston, Va., who reviewed and piloted parts of the text; Masako Kirihara, Osaka, Japan, Jane Stevenson, Modena, Italy, and Letizia Senni, Bologna, Italy, who reviewed parts of the text and made useful comments; Allen Ascher, senior acquisitions editor, and Christine Cervoni, production editor, at Addison Wesley Longman; and Kathy Sands-Boehmer, developmental editor, who deserves extra praise for working with us on all of our books.

Basic Reading Power

Copyright © 1997 by Addison Wesley Longman.

Addison Wesley Longman, 10 Bank Street, White Plains, NY 10606

Editorial director: Joanne Dresner
Senior acquisitions editor: Allen Ascher
Development editor: Kathy Sands-Boehmer
Production editor: Christine Cervoni
Cover design: Marshall Henrichs
Text design adaptation: Christine Gehring Wolf

Text art/Photos: pp. ix, 4, 7, 10-12, 16, 68, 87, 92, 112-116, 123, Daisy de Puthod; pp. 36-37, David Simonds, from *Simon and the Spy,* ©1995 by Addison Wesley Longman Ltd.; pp. 56-58, Trevor Clifford, from *English Works,* © 1993 by Addison Wesley Longman Ltd.; p. 49, excerpt from the *1996 Great Woods Popular Artist Series,* courtesy of Don Law Management.

Text credits: p. 37, excerpt from *Simon and the Spy,* by Elizabeth Laird. © 1995 by Addison Wesley Longman; p. 39, based on an idea from Charlotte Seeley; p. 62, excerpt from *Dead Man's River* by Elizabeth Laird. © 1990 by Addison Wesley Longman; p. 62, excerpt from *Tinker's Farm* by Stephen Rabley. ©1990 by Addison Wesley Longman; p. 63, excerpt from *Island for Sale* by Anne Collins. ©1992 by Addison Wesley Longman. All reprinted by permission of Addison Wesley Longman Ltd; p. 55, table of contents from *Making Business Decisions,* by Frances Boyd. © 1994 by Addison Wesley Longman. Reprinted by permission of Addison Wesley Longman.

ISBN: 0-201-84673-X

1 2 3 4 5 6 7 8 9 10—CRS—00 99 98 97 96

Contents

Dear Student:

Basic Reading Power can help you read well in English. In this book, you can work on reading in four ways:

1. Pleasure Reading
   Read many stories and books.

2. Comprehension Skills
   Understand what you read.

3. Vocabulary Building
   Learn many new words.

4. Thinking Skills
   Learn to think in English.

Work on all four parts of the book every week. This way you can learn to be a good reader!

Yours truly,

Beatrice Mikulecky

Linda Jeffries

Beatrice Mikulecky and Linda Jeffries

Questionnaire

➤ *Answer the questions. Then talk to other students about your answers.*

1. What is your name? _____

2. Where do you live? _____

3. What country do you come from? _____

4. What is your first language? _____

5. Do you like to read? _____

6. Do your parents or friends like to read? _____

7. What do you like to read?

   books _____   magazines _____

   newspapers _____   other _____

8. What do you read every day? _____

   books _____   magazines _____

   newspapers _____   other _____

9. How many books do you read in one year? _____

10. What book do you like a lot? _____

    _____

Vocabulary in *Basic Reading Power*

➤ *This exercise gives you some new words. These words are in the exercises in this book. Read the sentences. Can you do what they say?*

1. Draw a circle around the last word in this sentence.

2. There is a picture of a house below these sentences on the next page. Draw a circle around the house.

3. A word is missing from this _____. Write in the word.

4. There are two blanks in the next sentence. Think of some words. Write them in the blanks.

5. My _____ goes to _____ every day.

6. Draw a line from number 6 to number 1.

7. One word in this snetnece is not correct. Write that word correctly in the blank. _____

8. Cross out the first word in this sentence. Then cross out the last word in this sentence.

9. Draw a garden near the house below. Follow the steps in number 10.

10. Step 1. Draw a tree.

    Step 2. Draw some flowers.

    Step 3. Draw some grass.

➤ *Which words are new for you? Write them here.*

_____

_____

_____

_____

Part One

Pleasure Reading

Good readers read a lot of stories and books. They read for pleasure, not only for school or work. This part of the book is for pleasure reading. You are going to read and talk about many stories. You can learn to be a good reader in English.

Sometimes stories have a lot of new words. Do you have to know all the words? No!

Understanding a Story with Some New Words in It

➤ *1. Read the story. Then answer the questions.*

Magda is a student at Poznan University in Poland. She is 23 years old. She xxxxx in Mosina. It is a small xxxx near Poznan. Every day, Magda takes xxx train to the city. She goes xx her classes at the university. After her xxxxxxx, she studies with her friends. Sometimes, xxxx have dinner at a restaurant. Xxxx she takes the train home. She xxxxxxx all evening. She wants to be x doctor. She must study hard for xxxx years!

a. Does Magda live in Poznan? _____

b. Does she take the train to Poznan? _____

c. Does she always go home for dinner? _____

d. What is she studying? _____

➤ *2. Read the story. Then answer the questions.*

Gerald is a student at Harvard University in Cambridge, Massachusetts. He is 20 years old. Xx is from a small xxxx in California. He can't xx home very often. Gerald xx studying Chinese. He wants xx go to China next xxxx. In China he can learn Xxxxxxx well. He can also xxxxx about the country. Some xxx, Gerald wants to work xx business. He wants to xxx and sell things in Xxxxx. But first he must xxxxx how to speak Chinese.

a. Where is Gerald from? _____

b. Does he go home every weekend? _____

c. Can he speak Chinese? _____

d. Does he want to teach Chinese? _____

Reading to Understand Stories

Good readers think and ask questions when they read. Follow these steps with the story on the next page.

Step 1. Think before you read.

Look at any pictures.

Read the title of the story.

Can you answer any of these questions?

What is the story about?

Who is in the story?

Where are they?

Step 2. Read the story.

Do you have to know all the words? NO!

You can understand the story without all the words.

Don't ask the teacher or other students about new words.

Read to the end of the story.

Step 3. Talk about the story.

When you finish, talk about the story with another student.

What is the story about?

Who is in the story?

Where are they?

Do you like the story? Why?

Step 4. Learn new words.

Now look at the story again.

Find some new words.

Write the new words on the lines under the story.

Make a vocabulary list. (See pages 100–103.)

Fables

The stories in this unit are fables. Fables are short stories about people or animals. They are not true stories, but they give a lesson about life. Every country has its fables.

Fable 1

Step 1. Think before you read.

Step 2. Read the story.

The Big Family in the Little House

Vladimir does not know what to do. He has a big family. And he lives in a little house. He is not very happy.

One day he goes to town. He talks to a wise woman. "Please help me," he says. "My wife and I have six children. We live in a very
5   little house. Eight people in a few rooms! We cannot live this way!"

The wise woman listens. She closes her eyes for a minute. Then she asks, "How many animals do you have?"

"We have eight animals. We have a horse, a cow, two pigs, and four chickens," says Vladimir.

10 "Good. Go home now," says the wise woman. "Take all your animals into the house with you."

"Our animals!" says Vladimir. He goes home and does what the wise woman tells him. The next week, he goes back to the wise woman.

15 "This is very bad!" he says. "The animals eat our food. They fill all the rooms. They sleep in our beds."

The wise woman closes her eyes again. Then she tells Vladimir, "Now go home. Take the animals out of the house."

Vladimir goes home. He takes the animals out of the house.

20 The next day, he goes back to the wise woman. This time he is happy.

"Thank you, thank you," he says. "It's very different without the animals. Now we can eat. Now we can sleep. Now we like our house. Thank you for your help. You *are* a very wise woman!"

Step 3. Talk about the story. What is the lesson?

Step 4. Write new words here.

_____

_____

Fable 2

Step 1. Think before you read.

Step 2. Read the story.

That's Not the Way to Do It!

Hans wants to sell his horse. He goes down the road to town. He and his young son are walking with the horse. There are some boys near the road.

"That's not the way to do it!" says a boy. "Why is that man

5 walking? He has a horse!"

"He's right," says Hans. He gets on the horse. The son walks behind him. Then they see some women.

"Look at that man!" says a woman. "He is on the horse. And his poor boy must walk."

10 "She's right," says Hans. He gets off and he puts his son on the horse. They walk some more.

"Isn't that terrible!" says an old man. "Young people have no love for their parents! Look at that boy on the horse. His poor father is walking."

15 "He's right," says Hans. He gets on the horse behind his son. Then they see some girls.

"Two people on a horse!" say the girls. "The poor animal."

"They're right," says Hans. He and his son get off the horse. They take the horse in their arms. They carry him down the road.

20 The horse is big and he almost falls.

They come to a river with a bridge. Some people are on the bridge. "Look at that!" they say. "Look at the horse!" They laugh and laugh.

The horse does not like this. He moves here and there. He wants

25 to run away. "Help, help," cries Hans. And then they all fall off the bridge and into the river—the horse, Hans, and his son.

"Next time," says Hans, "I am not going to listen to other people. I am going to do it my way."

Step 3. Talk about the story. What is the lesson?

Step 4. Write new words here.

_____

_____

Fable 3

Step 1. Think before you read.

Step 2. Read the story.

The Wolf and the Dog

A wolf is looking for food. He is very hungry. One evening, he sees some chickens in a yard. He wants to eat those chickens. But there is a dog in the yard, too. The dog is very big and strong. The wolf does not want to fight the dog, but he is very, very hungry. He
5   waits near the yard.

The wolf sees a man come out of the house. The man gives some food to the dog. Then he goes back in the house.

"Good evening," the wolf calls to the dog.

"Good evening," answers the dog. He is eating his dinner.
10   The wolf says, "Do you get food every day?"

Veney

"Two times a day," answers the dog. "I get breakfast in the morning and dinner in the evening." He eats some more. Then he looks at the wolf. "Are you hungry? Come live here with me. This is a good life. I help the man a little. At night I sleep near the
15 chickens. No animals can get them."

The dog eats all his dinner and sits down. He says to the wolf, "You are always running and fighting. Your life is not easy. Come live here. Life is easy here."

The wolf sits down near the dog. He thinks, "Why not? I can eat
20 every day here, and I can have a friend."

But then he looks at the dog.

"What is that under your ears?" he asks.

"What?" says the dog.

"Look at your neck! It is all red!" says the wolf.

25 "Oh, that is nothing," says the dog.

"Nothing!" says the wolf. "It is terrible!"

"No, no," says the dog. "It is the chain. In the day, the farmer puts a chain on my neck."

"A chain!" says the wolf. "So you can't run. You must stay there
30 by the house all day!"

"Yes," answers the dog.

"Then no, thank you, my friend. I cannot stay here with you. I do not want a chain on my neck. I am going back to my old life. Good-bye!"

35 And the wolf runs away, still hungry.

Step 3. Talk about the story. What is the lesson?

Step 4. Write new words here.

_____

_____

Fable 4

Step 1. Think before you read.

Step 2. Read the story.

A Bell on the Cat

A large family of mice live in a store. There is always food in the store. Another family of mice comes to the store. Soon there are lots and lots of mice in the store.

5   The storekeeper is not happy about this. He says, "There are too many mice here!" So one day he goes out. He gets a big, black cat. It is hungry and it likes to eat mice.

The mice do not know what to do. "What can we do?" says a mother mouse. "This cat is terrible. It is going to kill us all."

"We must talk to our president. He always knows what to do,"
10 says another mouse. So they go to the president. "Mr. President," they say, "the cat is going to kill us. We are afraid. What can we do?"

The president is a big, old mouse. He says, "We must have a meeting. All the mice must come."

And so there is a meeting of all the mice. The president of the
15 mice comes in and stands up.

"My dear friends," he says, "we are living in a bad time. A big, black cat is here in our store. This terrible animal wants to eat us all. But my friends, I know what to do. Your president always has the answer. We can put a bell on the cat. That way we can always hear
20 it. And we can run away in time."

"Hurrah!" say all the mice. "Our president is very wise." The mice are all happy. They are all talking about their president. "Isn't he a wise mouse?" they say. "Isn't he a good president?"

But then a young mouse speaks. "Mr. President," she says, "I have
25 a question."

"Yes," says the president.

"Please," says the young mouse. "Who is going to put the bell on the cat?"

"Not I! Not I!" say all the mice. Then they stop talking. They all
30 go away. The next day, they move out of the store.

Step 3. Talk about the story. What is the lesson?

Step 4. Write new words here.

_____

_____

Fable 5

Step 1. Think before you read.

Step 2. Read the story.

The Boy and the Wolf

Kamal lives in a little village. Every day he goes out with his sheep. He stays with the sheep all day. In the evening he comes back to the village.

One day, the boy thinks, "I do not like this! I am with the sheep
5   all day. The sheep do not talk, and they do not listen to me. What can I do?"

Kamal sits there for some time. Then he says, "I know!" And he cries, "Wolf! Wolf!"

In a few minutes, people come running from the village.
10   "Where is the wolf?" they ask.

"Oh, there is no wolf," says the boy. "I wanted to see you and talk to you."

The people are not happy. They go back to the village. "That bad boy!" they say.

15   The next day, Kamal is with his sheep. Again, he does not want to be alone. He cries, "Wolf! Wolf!"

Again, the people come from the village. This time, they are very angry. "You must not do that again!" they say. "Next time, we are not going to listen." And they go back to their work.

20   That same afternoon, Kamal is alone with his sheep. He is almost asleep. Then he hears something in the trees. He opens his eyes. It is a wolf. The wolf is coming to eat his sheep.

"Help! Help!" cries Kamal. "There is a wolf!"

The people in the village hear the boy, but this time they do not
25 come.

So Kamal runs away, and the wolf kills and eats all the sheep.

Step 3. Talk about the story. What is the lesson?

Step 4. Write new words here.

_____

_____

Fable 6

Step 1. Think before you read.

Step 2. Read the story.

The Bear and the Two Friends

One day, Dan and Jim walked down the road.

"What a beautiful day!" said Dan.

"Yes, this is a good day for a walk," said Jim. "It is not raining, and it is not hot."

5 So they talked and walked. They walked and talked. They came to a mountain with lots of trees. Then Jim stopped talking. There was a

bear behind a tree. Jim said nothing to Dan. In a minute, Jim was up in a tree. Then he called to his friend, "Oh Dan, there is a bear!"

10   Dan did not have time to run. He did not have time to go up a tree. So he fell to the ground. He did not move.

    The bear walked over to him and smelled him. He made noises in Dan's ear. Dan still did not move. After some time, the bear went away. Bears do not eat dead people or animals.

    Then Jim came down from the tree.

15   "Sorry," he said. "I wanted to tell you about the bear. But first, I wanted to get up the tree."

    Dan said nothing. He got up from the ground.

    "What did the bear say to you?" asked Jim.

    "He told me something very important," said Dan.

20   "Oh, what was that?" asked Jim.

    "He told me about good friends. Good friends do not run away. Good friends help their friends."

    And Dan walked down the road alone.

Step 3. Talk about the story. What is the lesson?

Step 4. Write new words here.

_____

_____

Fable 7

Step 1. Think before you read.

Step 2. Read the story.

Sinbad and the Genie

One day, Sinbad the Sailor was by the sea. He sat down by the water. Somebody called to him. There was an old bottle near him. He looked at the bottle. In it, there was a very, very little person. It was a genie.

5 "Help! Help!" said the genie. "Please let me out."

Sinbad opened the bottle. A big, gray cloud came out. In the cloud, there was a very, very big genie.

"Thank you, Sailor. And now, I am going to eat you. My last meal was 5,000 years ago. I am very hungry."

10 The genie was very big and strong, and he had Sinbad in his hand. Sinbad was small and not very strong. But he was clever.

He said to the genie, "How can you eat me—a little thing like you?"

"Little?" said the genie, in a terrible way. "I am very big!"

15 "How can you be very big?" asked Sinbad. "You were in this little bottle!"

"I changed," said the genie. "You can see that!"

"No, no," said Sinbad. "I see only a little bottle."

The genie's face was all red. He was very terrible to see. "I can
20 change!" he said. "Look at me!"

The genie went into his big, gray cloud. Then the cloud went away. The genie was little, and he was inside the bottle again.

Sinbad put the top on the bottle. He put the bottle in the sea and walked away. "Good-bye for another 5,000 years!" Sinbad said.

Step 3. Talk about the story. What is the lesson?

Step 4. Write new words here.

_____

_____

Fable 8

Step 1. Think before you read.

Step 2. Read the story.

The Strongest Person

Mariko was a girl mouse. She loved Nazumi, a boy mouse. They wanted to marry. But Mariko's parents said no. Mariko must marry the strongest person in the world. But who was the strongest person in the world?

5   Her parents looked up at the sky. "The sun is the strongest person," they said. They asked the sun, "Do you want to marry our daughter?"

"Your daughter is very beautiful," said the sun. "But I'm not the strongest person. The cloud is stronger. He can stop my light."

10   So Mariko's parents called to the cloud. "Are you the strongest person?" they asked.

The cloud answered, "No, no. I'm not the strongest person. The wind is stronger. I must go where he tells me."

"Oh, Wind," said Mariko's parents. "What do you say? Are you 15 very strong?"

"Yes, yes," said the wind. "I'm very strong. But a high wall can stop me."

The mice parents talked to a high wall. "Please, Wall, can you answer our question? We are looking for the strongest person in the 20 world. Are you that person?"

The wall said, "I'm very strong. But look at my feet. There are many holes. Nazumi, the mouse, made those holes."

Mariko's parents looked at the holes. Then they went to look for Nazumi. "Nazumi," they said, "you are the strongest person in the 25 world! Do you want to marry our daughter?"

"Yes," said Nazumi. And so Mariko married Nazumi, and they were very happy.

Step 3. Talk about the story. What is the lesson?

Step 4. Write new words here.

_____

_____

Fable 9

Step 1. Think before you read.

Step 2. Read the story.

The Turtle and the Ducks

The turtle was not very happy. "Here I am on the ground," he said. "I cannot go fast. I always see the same things. I see only the ground and the grass. Poor, poor me."

Then the turtle looked up at the sky. "Look at those birds," he
5 said. "They go many places. They see many things. I want to be a bird. I want to fly, too."

Two ducks stopped near the turtle.

"Oh, ducks," asked the turtle. "What can I do? I want to go to far places. I want to see the world."

10 "I think we can help you," said the ducks.

"Can you?" asked the turtle. "How?"

"You can fly with us to Africa or to America. You can see mountains, oceans, and cities—all the things you want to see."

"But how can I fly?" asked the turtle.

15 "With a stick," said the ducks. "We can hold the stick in our mouths. And you must hold on with your mouth."

And that's what they did. They went up in the air. They went many miles. The turtle saw many new things. He saw a city and lots of people.

20 Some people on the ground looked up. "A turtle in the air!" they said. "Run, run to the queen. There is a flying turtle. She must see it."

The queen came out to see the turtle. "Where is it?" she asked.

"Here! Can't you see me?" called the turtle. But when he opened his mouth, he fell to the ground. And there, in front of the queen
25 and all the people, he died.

Step 3. Talk about the story. What is the lesson?

Step 4. Write new words here.

_____

_____

Fable 10

Step 1. Think before you read.

Step 2. Read the story.

The Fisherman and His Wife

Once there was a fisherman. He and his wife lived in a little house. They were very poor.

One day he went to the sea. He wanted to get some fish for dinner. For many hours, he got nothing. Then, in the evening, he got a big, fat fish.

"Please don't eat me!" said the fish. "Tell me what you want. I can give it to you."

The fisherman put the fish back into the sea. He went home and told his wife about the fish. She said, "Husband! I don't like this old house. Tell the fish I want a new house."

So the fisherman went back to the sea. He called to the fish, "Oh, fish! My wife wants a new house!"

"Go home," said the fish. "Your wife has a new house."

The fisherman went home. His wife was in a nice, new house. There were flowers in the yard, and she was very happy.

But the next morning, she was not happy. She said to her husband, "This house is very small. I want a big house now. Go back to the fish and tell him."

So the fisherman went back to the sea. "Oh, fish!" he called.
20   "My wife wants a big house now."

"Go home," said the fish. "Your wife has a big house."

The fisherman went home. There was his wife in a very big and beautiful house. She was very happy.

But the next morning she said, "A big house is nice. But it is not
25   enough. I want to be a queen!"

So the fisherman went back to the sea again. "Oh, fish!" he called. "My wife wants to be a queen now."

"Go home," said the fish. "Your wife is a queen."

The fisherman went home. His wife was now a queen. She had
30   on a beautiful dress. "Now you can be happy," said the fisherman to his wife.

The next morning it rained. The fisherman's wife said, "I don't like the rain. Tell the fish. I want to stop the rain."

So the fisherman went back to the sea another time. "Oh, fish!"
35   he called. "Help me! My wife is still not happy. She wants to stop the rain."

"Go home," said the fish. "Your wife asks for too much! Now she has nothing."

The fisherman went home. His wife was in their old house
40   again. And once again, they were very poor.

Step 3. Talk about the story. What is the lesson?

Step 4. Write new words here.

_____

_____

Stories

The stories in this unit are not fables. They are all about real people and places.

Remember the Four Reading Steps

- Think before you read.
- Read the story.
- Talk about the story.
- Learn new words.

Story 1

A Very Special Party

Amalya Antonovna lived in St. Petersburg, Russia. She was 75 years old, and she was alone. Her husband was dead. She had a son, Pavel, but maybe he was also dead. She last saw him in 1945. After that, she did not hear anymore about him.

5   What happened in 1945? That was a time of war in Europe. Pavel's father was a soldier. He was killed in the war in 1942. After that, Amalya was alone with her baby. Those were terrible times in Russia. There was very little food. The winter was very cold. The German army was in Russia. German soldiers killed many Russians.

10   They sent many other Russians to Germany to work. Many of these people got sick and died.

Amalya was a Russian worker in Germany. At the end of the war, she was still alive. Her baby was still alive, too. But Amalya was very sick. The English and American armies came to the town. Amalya

15   asked some English soldiers for help. "Take my little boy," she said. "I am very sick, but he must live."

So Pavel went to England. He went to live with an English family, the Corbetts. He was just two years old. Grace and George Corbett were very good to Pavel. He was a son for them. They gave him an
20 English name—Paul. They never told him about his Russian mother.

Paul Corbett married and had two children. When he was 45, Grace Corbett died. Then George Corbett told him about his Russian mother. Paul wanted to look for her. Maybe she was dead after all these years. But maybe not.

25 He sent many letters to Russia. Several years passed. Then one day a letter came from St. Petersburg. Amalya was alive and well, and she wanted very much to see him. So Paul Corbett went with his family to St. Petersburg.

Amalya had a big party. All her friends came to meet her son.
30 There was lots of good Russian food and music. Amalya did not speak any English. Paul and his family did not speak any Russian. But words were not important. They were all happy.

Story 2

Christmas Gifts

Christmas was a big day for John and Adele. They always had a very nice dinner. Then they opened their presents. Often the presents were small things. John and Adele did not have much money. But John always had something for Adele, and Adele always
5 had something for John.

It was the day before Christmas. But this year John and Adele still did not have any presents. They did not have any money for presents. "We are happy without them," they said.

But it was not true. John wanted to buy something for his wife.
10 And Adele wanted to buy something for her husband.

Adele went into town. She looked at the store windows. There were many beautiful things in the windows. In the window of a music store, she saw some cassettes. There was a new cassette by Pavarotti. John loved music, and he loved Pavarotti. Adele wanted
15 to buy that cassette for John, but she did not have the money.

Then she remembered her hair. Adele had very long, beautiful red hair. Her hairdresser wanted to cut it and buy it from her. Adele always said no. But now she went to the hairdresser and said yes.

Then she went back to the music store with the money, and she
20 bought the Pavarotti cassette.

When Adele came home, John was already there.

"What do you think?" Adele asked him. "Do you like my new Christmas haircut?"

"Oh no!" John said.

25 "You don't like it?" Adele said.

"Why did you do that?" John asked.

"I wanted to buy something for you," said Adele. "So I sold my hair. Here is your present."

John opened the present. "Oh, Adele!" he said. "This is terrible!"

30 "You mean you don't like the cassette?" asked Adele.

"No, no. Thank you. It's a beautiful cassette," said John. "But I don't have a cassette player now. I needed money for your present, and my friend George needed a cassette player. So I sold the cassette player to him. Here's your present."

35 Adele opened a small box. In it there were two combs for her hair. They were very beautiful, but now her hair was very short. She couldn't use combs!

"I can use them next year," she said. "Thank you, my love."

"And someday soon I'm going to get another cassette player,"
40 John said. He smiled. "You know, Adele, you're beautiful with short hair!"

Story 3

The Telephone Call

Camille was three years old. She lived in a small town in France. Her father worked far away in the city. Her mother worked in the house.

One Saturday, Camille's mother fell down on the floor. Her eyes
5 were closed. She did not move. Camille's father was home. He called the doctor on the telephone. The doctor came to help Camille's mother. In a few days, she was well.

Then one day she fell down again. This time, Camille's father was not home. There was only Camille. She looked at her mother on the
10 floor, and she was afraid. She started to cry. Then she remembered the telephone. She went to the telephone. She did the same thing her father did. She pushed some numbers on the telephone.

A man answered her call. He was Claude Armand, an engineer. His office was in the city. He did not know Camille. At first, he did
15 not understand her.

Camille said, "Mommy, Mommy!"

"Where is your mother?" asked Claude Armand.

"She's lying down," said Camille. "She can't get up." Camille started to cry.

20 Claude Armand wanted to help Camille. "Where do you live?" he asked.

"Near my grandma," she answered. She didn't know her street or her town. She was only three!

Then Claude Armand said to her, "Don't put down the telephone. Talk to me some more. Tell me about your daddy. Where is he?"

25

He asked her lots of questions. At the same time, a friend in his office called the telephone company. She told the telephone company about Camille's mother. She said they needed Camille's address. The telephone company told the police. The police told the government in Paris. Then the government said okay to the police. The police said okay to the telephone company. And the telephone company told them Camille's address.

30

All this time, Camille talked with Claude Armand. She told him about her house and her family. She told him about her grandparents, her friends, and her little cat. They talked for 45 minutes!

35

Then the police were at Camille's house with a doctor. They called to her and rang the doorbell. Camille said good-bye to Claude Armand and went to open the door. Now she was not alone anymore. Now her mother was okay.

40

Story 4

What's in the Back Seat?

It was a cold day in Chicago. Laura Simon had no more milk in her refrigerator. She put the baby in the car, and she drove to the store. It was only ten minutes away. But in five minutes, the baby was asleep.

5 Laura stopped in front of the store. She looked at the sleeping baby. She did not want to wake him up. But she also did not want him to get cold. There was a coat on the back seat. She put it over the baby. Then she went into the store. The car key was still in the car.

10   Todd Jenkins walked by. He saw the key in Laura Simon's car. He was cold, and he did not want to walk. He got in the car and drove away.

    After five minutes, there was a noise in the car. What was that? Todd drove some more. Then he stopped. There was something in the car. He looked at the back seat and saw a coat. The noise came
15 from under the coat. He moved the coat, and there was a baby!

    Todd looked at the baby. The baby looked at him and smiled. "Daa Daa," said the baby.

    "No, I'm not your daddy," said Todd. He got out of the car and walked away. Then he looked back. The baby started to cry. Todd
20 went back to the car. The baby stopped crying and smiled again. "Daa Daa," he said again.

    Todd got back in the car and drove some more. The baby was happy. But after a few minutes, he started to cry again. "Waa waa," he said.

25   "What do you want?" asked Todd.

    "Waa waa," said the baby.

    "Are you hungry?" asked Todd.

    The baby stopped crying.

    "I don't have any milk," said Todd. "Now what can I do? He's
30 hungry!"

    Todd looked at the baby. The baby looked at Todd.

    "Waa waa!" said the baby again.

    "Okay, okay," Todd said. He drove back to the store. Laura Simon was there. A policeman and policewoman were there, too.

35   Todd Jenkins got out of the car. "I think your baby is hungry," he said to Laura Simon.

    "My poor baby!" said Laura Simon, and she ran to the car.

    "Never again!" said Todd Jenkins to the police, and they took him away.

Story 5

A Day Trip to Mexico

    Seattle is a city by the sea. There are lots of boats in Seattle. Some of the boats are fishing boats. Some boats go to far places. Some boats go to the San Juan Islands near by.

5 Anthony Brewer lived in Seattle. He was sixteen, and he wanted to go away. It was the end of the school year, and it was hot. Anthony's friends were on the San Juan Islands. He wanted to go there, too.

One morning, Anthony had an idea. He didn't tell his parents about his idea. They were at work. He went down to the boats. He 10 wanted to buy a ticket for the San Juan Islands. But he did not have very much money. He walked by the boats. It was early, and there were not many people. Then he walked onto a boat. There were some large boxes on the boat. He got into a box and closed it.

There was a hole in the box. Anthony looked through the hole, 15 and he saw some men come onto the boat. Then the boat started to move. Anthony saw the buildings of Seattle, and then he saw only the sea.

It was a warm day. Anthony was happy in the box. The boat moved up and down a little. Soon he was asleep. He slept for two 20 hours. Two hours! Why were they still at sea? The San Juan Islands were only an hour from Seattle. He looked out and saw only the sea all around. He listened to the people on the boat, but he could not understand them. Maybe this wasn't the boat for the San Juan Islands! What boat was it? Where was it going?

25 Anthony didn't know what to do. He sat in the box all day. Night came and it was very cold in the box. He had no warm clothing, no food, and nothing to drink. Now he wanted to go home!

The next morning, some men opened the box. They saw 30 Anthony, and they pulled him out. Anthony was afraid. But the men smiled, and they gave him some food and some water.

"Where is the boat going?" he asked.

"To Mexico," they answered.

"Can you stop before that?" he asked. "I have to go home!"

35 "No," they said. "We can't stop. But we can call your parents on the radio."

Ten days later, Anthony was in Mexico. He went to the Mexican police for help. They put him on a plane to Seattle. His parents came to get him at the airport. The airplane ticket cost them $500, 40 but they were not angry. They were happy to see Anthony again.

"I wanted to go away," said Anthony, "but not to Mexico! I only wanted to go on a day trip."

Story 6

Young Love

In 1942, Italy was at war. Antonio was a soldier in the Italian army. He was in a small city in Tunisia. In this city, there was a hotel. The manager of the hotel was Italian.

Antonio often went to the hotel. He was a friend of the manager
5   and his family. He liked to talk with them about Italy and about the end of the war. The manager's daughter, Sabrina, was 19. She was very beautiful. Antonio liked her very much and wanted to talk with her, but she did not like to talk to soldiers.

So Antonio watched her and waited. Then, one day, she smiled
10 at him. He smiled at her, and they started talking. They talked and talked. In a short time, they were in love, and they wanted to get married. But her parents said, "You can't get married now because there is war. You must wait."

Soon the war was close to the city. One day, Antonio went to see
15 Sabrina. He was very sad. "I must leave tomorrow with the army," he said. "The British army is going to be here soon."

Sabrina cried and cried. Antonio cried, too. He was at the hotel with Sabrina and her family all night. He went away with the first light. Antonio and Sabrina stopped at the door for a last kiss. Then
20 he walked away. At the end of the street, he looked back. Sabrina was still there at the door.

The war did not go well for the Italian army. The British army took many Italian soldiers with them. Antonio was one of these soldiers. The English sent him to India. He was there for four years.

25 Antonio sent many letters to Sabrina, but the letters all came back to him. Where was Sabrina? Was she still alive? He did not get any answers to his questions.

Then, in 1946, Antonio went back to Italy. He went to work in Milan. He got married, and soon he had two children. One day, in
30 1961, he was in Rome, and he saw Sabrina in a store. He went into the store.

At first, she was happy to see him, but then she cried. They went into a cafe and had some coffee. Sabrina now lived in Rome. She was married and had three children. She was happy with her life.
35 "But," she said, "I waited for many years. I waited for you."

It was time for Antonio to get his train back to Milan. They went out into the street and said good-bye. Antonio went back to his family in Milan, and Sabrina went back to her family in Rome. Antonio never saw Sabrina again.

Story 7

Man's Best Friend

Rudy was a large, brown dog. He was from Hamburg, Germany, but he was not at home very often. He was in a truck on the roads of Europe.

Rudy did not drive the truck. His friend, Heinrich, was the driver. Rudy and Heinrich often lived in the truck for many days. They stopped at restaurants for their meals. They had beds on the truck. On long drives, Heinrich did not want to fall asleep. So he talked to Rudy and Rudy listened.

In Hamburg, they lived with Heinrich's sister, Elena. At home, Heinrich and Rudy liked to sleep a lot. They also went for long walks, or they went to see Heinrich's friends. Rudy always went with Heinrich.

One evening, Rudy and Heinrich did not come home. In the morning, Elena called Heinrich's friends. They did not know about Heinrich. Then there was a noise at the door. Elena opened the door, and there was Rudy. He was alone. He barked at her and wanted her to go out with him. Elena called the police. After some time, the police called her back. Heinrich was in the hospital. It was his heart. He was very sick.

Elena went to the hospital to see her brother. His eyes were closed, and he did not talk. The doctor said Heinrich was not in danger anymore but was still very sick.

The next day, Heinrich opened his eyes. He asked about Rudy. Poor Rudy. He was at home, waiting for Heinrich. He waited and waited by the door. He did not want to get up, and he did not want to eat. Elena called the animal doctor. The doctor looked at Rudy and said, "This dog is not sick. He's sad."

Elena told Heinrich about Rudy. Heinrich said, "Give Rudy my hat."

Elena went home with the hat. Rudy put his nose to the hat. He moved his tail. He ate some food and got up from the floor. But he did not move away from the door. The next day he stopped eating again.

Then Elena went to Heinrich's doctor. She told him about Rudy. "Can I bring Rudy to the hospital?" she asked.

"No," said the doctor. "No dogs in the hospital." The doctor was sorry for Rudy. He talked to some other doctors. In the end, they said, "Okay. There's a little room near the hospital door. Rudy can meet Heinrich in that room."

40   Elena went to the hospital with Rudy. He was very thin, and he walked very slowly. But when he saw Heinrich, he jumped up and barked and barked. Heinrich was on a bed. He smiled and talked to Rudy. And after that, Rudy started to eat again. He started to run and play again.

Story 8

A Man and Many Wolves

      Farley Mowat worked for the Canadian government. The government wanted to know more about wolves. Do wolves kill lots of caribou (big animals)? Do they kill people? The government told Farley to learn about wolves.

5   They gave him lots of food and clothes and guns. Then they put him on a plane and took him to a far place. The plane put him down and went away. There were no houses or people in this place. But there were lots of animals—and lots of wolves.

      People tell terrible stories about wolves. They say wolves like to
10   kill and eat people. Farley remembered these stories, and he was afraid. He had his gun with him all the time.

      Then one day, he saw a group of wolves. There was a mother wolf with four baby wolves. A father wolf and another young wolf lived with them.

15   Farley watched these wolves every day. The mother was a very good mother. She gave milk to her babies. She gave them lessons about life. They learned how to get food. The father wolf got food for the mother. The young wolf played with the children. They were a nice, happy family—a wolf family!

20   Farley did not need his gun anymore. In a short time, he and the wolf family were friends. Farley watched them for five months. He learned many new things about wolves. He learned that many stories about wolves were not true. Wolves do not eat people, and they do not eat many large animals.

25   What do they eat? Lots of small animals, Farley learned. For example, they eat lots and lots of mice. Can a large animal live on mice? Farley wanted to know. There was only one way to learn. He was a large animal, too—a large man. He must try to live on mice! So he did. He ate mice—and no other food—for two weeks. After
30   that, he did not want any more mice! But he was not thin, and he

was not sick. Yes, a man can live on mice, so a wolf can, too. Now he could answer the government's questions about wolves.

35   In that far place, Farley did not see many people. But he learned bad things about some men. These men told terrible stories about wolves. In the stories, wolves killed hundreds of caribou. But this was not true. Farley learned that the men killed the caribou. They also killed many wolves.

    Farley Mowat never saw the wolf family again. But he wrote a book about them. He wanted people to understand wolves and to
40   stop killing them.

Story 9

Ben and Jerry's

    Ben Cohen and Jerry Greenfield were good friends in high school. They came from Merrick, New York. After college, they wanted to start a business. What kind of business? A food business, of course. Ben and Jerry were different in many ways, but in one
5   way they were the same. They liked food!

    One food they liked very much was ice cream. They wanted to open an ice-cream shop. Where was a good place for an ice-cream shop? They looked at many cities and towns. Then they went to Burlington, Vermont. They liked the city a lot. It had lots of young
10   people, and it did not have any good ice-cream shops. There was only one problem with Burlington. For four months of the year, it was cold there. Did people buy ice cream on cold days?

    On May 5, 1978, Ben and Jerry opened their ice-cream shop. It was a small shop, and it was not very beautiful. But the ice cream
15   was very good. Lots of people came to eat ice cream on opening day. They came back again and again. There were always lots of people in the shop. Ben and Jerry worked very hard. One night after work, Ben was very tired. He went to sleep on the ground in front of the shop!

20   After a few months, Ben and Jerry went to the bank. They had bad news. There were only a few dollars in their bank account.

    "Why is that?" they asked. "After all those months of hard work!"

    Then they started to learn about business. They learned about costs and expenses. And they learned about marketing and sales.
25   They started to have big ice-cream parties. They gave free ice cream

on some days. People in other cities learned about Ben and Jerry's, and they came a long way to eat the ice cream.

Ben and Jerry made more ice cream, and they started selling it to stores and restaurants. First, they went to stores and restaurants 30 in Vermont. Then they started selling their ice cream to stores across the United States. By 1988, they were selling ice cream all over the United States. A few years later, people could also buy their ice cream in Canada, Great Britain, Russia, and Israel.

Why do people buy Ben and Jerry's ice cream? First of all, it is 35 very, very good ice cream. It is made with good Vermont milk, and it does not have any chemicals in it. People also buy Ben and Jerry's ice cream because they like the company. It is now a very big company, but Ben and Jerry are not just big businessmen. They also want to help people in many different ways. They give work to lots 40 of poor people. And every year, the company gives away 7.5 percent of their money. They give money to help children and sick people in the United States and in other countries.

Story 10

Read a Book—or Go to Jail!

Stan Rosen lived in New Bedford, Massachusetts. He stole cars and bicycles from people. One day, the police saw him and sent him to jail. The next year, Stan was out of jail. He told some people his name was Jim Rosen. He got money from them for a business. 5 Then he ran away with the money. The police got him again and sent him to jail. The year after that, Stan was home again. One night, he stole some money from a store, and again, the police got him. But this time, they sent him to Judge Kane.

Judge Kane asked Stan, "Do you want to go to jail again? Or do 10 you want to read books?"

Stan did not understand.

"This time," said the judge, "you can decide. You can read books with Professor Waxler at the New Bedford high school. Or you can go to jail."

15 Stan was 27 years old. He did not have a high school degree. He did not often read books, and he did not like reading! But he did not want to go to jail again. So he decided to read books in Professor Waxler's class.

20 "You must go to every class," said Judge Kane. "And you must read all the books."

One evening, Stan went to the first class. There were ten men in the class, and all of the men were sent by Judge Kane. In the first class, they read a short story.

Professor Waxler asked, "What did you think about it?"

25 The men said nothing. They did not know how to talk about stories. Stan wanted to answer the question, but he was afraid to talk. He did not want the other men to hear him.

"Did you like the story?" Professor Waxler asked him.

"No," said Stan.

30 "Why not?" asked Professor Waxler.

"Because the end was happy, but life is not happy," said Stan.

"That's not true," said another man. "Life is happy for some people."

Then other men started talking about the story and about life.
35 They talked for two hours. Professor Waxler told them to read a book for the next class. It was a book about a young man with many problems.

Again, Professor Waxler asked, "What did you think?"

This time the men were not afraid to answer. They had lots of
40 ideas about the book, and they talked a lot about their lives.

For 12 weeks, Stan read books and talked about them. Then he had to decide again: go to class or go to jail. He decided to go to class again.

After that, Stan took evening classes at the high school. He went
45 to work in the daytime. The next year, he started evening classes at the university. Now Stan is a good student—and a good man. No more police or jail in Stan's life! Thanks to Judge Kane and Professor Waxler—and some books.

Story 11

Who Took the Money?

Manuel lived in a village in Spain called Santa Maria. It was a small village in the mountains. At 15, Manuel started working on the Spanish trains. Every Monday morning, he went by train down to the city. He came back home again on Friday evening. He worked
5 for long hours, and he worked hard.

When he was 24, he married Maria. She was from the next village. They had two daughters, Sofia and Lucinda. Manuel did not see his family very much. He was away for five days a week. But he had a good job, and that was important.

10   Santa Maria was a poor village. Many men there did not have good jobs. They worked only a few months every year. Their families did not have money for meat or coffee. Their children did not have good coats or shoes. But Manuel's daughters always had good coats and shoes. The family had meat, coffee, and other good

15   things to eat. On Sundays, Sofia and Lucinda had ice cream after dinner.

But not all Manuel's money went to his family. Every month, he put a little money in the bank. He did not tell Maria about this.

"A little money in the bank is important," he thought. "But

20   money can be a bad thing. People can get angry and fight about money. I'm not going to tell my wife and daughters about this money. Not now. Someday I can tell them, and we can do something special. We can all go stay in a hotel by the sea."

Year after year, Manuel put a little money in the bank. His

25   daughters got married and moved to the city. Sofia married Ruiz, and they had two children, a girl and a boy. Lucinda married Carlos, and they had a girl. On weekends, Sofia and Lucinda often went back to the village with their children. The children liked the village, and they loved Manuel and Maria. They played in the garden with the

30   dog and the cat. They went with Manuel in the mountains to get flowers and fruit. Maria cooked big meals for them and made them warm clothes.

When Manuel was 65, he stopped working. Now he did not go to the city every week. He stayed in the village with his wife. He

35   worked in the garden, and he took care of his fruit trees. He walked a lot in the mountains, and sometimes he sat with his friends in the cafe. They drank coffee, talked, and played cards. He still got money every month from the government, and he still put a little money in the bank.

40   "Soon I can tell Maria and the girls about my money," he thought. "And next summer we can all go to the seaside."

But Manuel and Maria always had lots of things to do. There was the house and the garden, the dog and the cat, and the grandchildren. They went to school in the city now. But sometimes

45   they were sick, and sometimes there was no school. Then they stayed with Manuel and Maria.

One day, Manuel's wife did not feel very well. She went to bed, and Manuel called the doctor. The doctor said it was nothing. But after a week, she still did not feel well. The doctor sent her to the

50   hospital in the city. The hospital doctors did some tests. They told

the family she was very sick. Manuel, Lucinda, and Sofia stayed with her night and day in the hospital. A month went by and Maria did not get better. The doctors then said she was going to die.

Sofia and Lucinda drove her home to the village. She lived for a few more weeks. Manuel stayed with her all the time. The daughters came often. And then, one day, she said good-bye to Manuel and she died.

Lucinda and Sofia stayed with Manuel for a week after that. They put away all Maria's clothes and things. They cleaned the house and cooked. Then they went back to the city, back to their families and their jobs.

Now Manuel was alone. Some women in the village said, "We can help you in the house. We can make dinner for you and wash your clothes. You do not have to pay us very much."

Manuel said no, he did not want help. He did not want other women in his house. He also did not want to pay these women. He had money in the bank, but it was not for the village women.

Some years went by. Manuel learned how to cook and how to wash his clothes. His house was always clean, and his garden was full of fruit and vegetables. Now his grandchildren did not come very often because they had to study on the weekends. His daughters said, "Why don't you come live in the city with us?"

But Manuel did not want to leave his home. Now he did not even want to go to the seaside. He did not want to go away without Maria. He was 77 years old. On some days, he felt very old and tired. Then he liked to sit in his garden with his cat and his dog. Of course, these were not the same cat and dog. They were the first cat's and dog's children's children!

One day, Manuel looked at the cat and the dog. Now they were old, too. The dog never barked, and the cat never ran after mice. "We are all old now," Manuel said to them. "We are all going to die before long. Then who is going to have my money? I don't want the bank to have it! I must go and get it."

So, one morning, Manuel went to the bank. He asked for all his money. The bank manager came and talked to Manuel. He said, "What are you going to do with this money? You have $30,000. You can't walk home with $30,000!"

Manuel said, "It's my money. I can do what I want." He put the money in a bag and went home. At home, he put the money under his bed. He did not want people to find it. But that night he did not sleep well. When the cat came into his room, he said, "Who's that?" and jumped out of bed.

"This is no good," he said. "I can't live with all this money in my house."

95   In the morning, he went out to the garden. He made a big hole under a plum tree. He put the bag of money in the hole. He put dirt back in the hole, and he put grass on top. Every day, he looked at that place under the plum tree. He often thought about the money, and he thought about his daughters and grandchildren. But the

100   money stayed under the plum tree, because there was a problem. Manuel couldn't decide about the money. He had $30,000, and he had two daughters. He could give $15,000 to each daughter. But Sofia had two children and Lucinda had only one. So that was not good. He could give money only to the grandchildren. He could

105   give them $10,000 each. But that meant no money for his daughters. He couldn't do that!

        The winter went by. Spring came and there were lots of flowers on the plum tree. Manuel still couldn't decide about his money. Summer came and Manuel's garden was full of fruit and vegetables. But the

110   plum tree had very few plums and those plums were not sweet.

        "I think the tree is telling me something," said Manuel. "Money must not stay in a hole in the ground."

        He telephoned his daughters. "Please come this weekend," he said. "I have something important to tell you."

115   Sofia and Lucinda came on Friday evening with their families. Sofia's girl, Yolanda, was now 20 years old and Pablo was 17. Lucinda's girl, Julia, was l8. Yolanda was a university student. She wanted to be a doctor. Pablo and Julia were high school students. Pablo wanted to be a writer and Julia wanted to be a

120   policewoman.

        At dinner that evening, Manuel said nothing about the money. Lucinda looked at Sofia, and Sofia looked at her father. They talked about the city and the government. They talked about the village and the garden. Yolanda, Pablo, and Julia went for a walk around

125   the village. "What is he going to tell us?" they asked. But Manuel told them nothing that evening, and they all went to bed.

        At breakfast the next morning, Manuel said, "Now it is day. Now I am ready. Come with me to the garden."

        Manuel went to the plum tree and stopped. "I am getting old,"

130   he said. "I'm going to die before long. I want to give you something."

        He took the grass away from the hole. He took out the dirt. "Oh, no!" he cried.

        "What is it?" asked his daughters.

135   "Look!" he said. "Look at that hole. It's empty!" Manuel sat down on the grass. "Who took it?" he cried. "Who took it?"

        "Who took what?" asked Sofia and Lucinda.

        "My money!" said Manuel.

140 "Your money?!" they asked. "Why did you put money in the ground? Money must stay in the bank!"

"I didn't want them to have my money. It was my money," said Manuel. "I wanted to give it to you."

"How much was it?" asked Sofia.

"$30,000," said Manuel.

145 "$30,000!" said Sofia and Lucinda. "You put all that money in a hole in the ground!"

Poor Manuel. He sat on the ground with his head in his hands.

"We must go to the police!" said Ruiz.

"Yes, we must tell them," said Carlos. "Maybe they can find the

150 thief."

So Ruiz, Carlos, Sofia, and Lucinda ran to the police. Yolanda, Pablo, and Julia stayed with Manuel in the garden. Julia looked in the hole. She put her hands in and pulled out some very small pieces of paper.

155 "Look!" she said. "Look at these."

"Pieces of money!" said Pablo.

"Why in little pieces?" asked Yolanda. "What kind of thief does that?"

"I think there were many thieves," said Julia.

160 "Why do you say that?" asked Pablo.

"There were many small thieves," said Julia.

"Children!" said Yolanda. "That's terrible! Village children!"

"No, not children," said Julia. "Very, very small thieves. They *ate* the money."

165 "What do you mean?" asked Pablo.

"Look in the hole," said Julia. "Do you see those little black things? What makes little black things? What eats paper?"

"Mice!!!" said Pablo and Yolanda.

"Yes, mice," said Julia.

170 Manuel looked up.

"It's true," he said. "There are lots of mice. The cat is old and she doesn't run after them now."

Manuel looked at Yolanda, Pablo, and Julia. "I'm very sorry," he said. "I wanted to give you that money. I wanted to send you to the

175 seaside. I wanted . . ." He stopped.

The cat came out and sat down near Manuel. She was black and white and very fat.

"Where were you?" said Julia to the cat. "Why weren't you out here at work?"

180 "Miao!" said the cat.

"Were you asleep in the house?" asked Julia.

"Miao," said the cat.

Then Pablo started to laugh. "Think about it," he said. "$30,000! Those mice ate $30,000!"

185   Yolanda and Julia also started to laugh.

"What are the police going to do?" said Pablo. "Take the mice to jail?"

Yolanda, Pablo, and Julia laughed more and more. They fell on the ground laughing. Manuel looked at them.

190   He thought, "How can they laugh? That was years of work, that money."

He listened to his grandchildren, still laughing and talking. And then he thought, "Maybe they're right. Why cry? I can't get the money back now."

195   And he smiled sadly at the cat.

Reading Books for Pleasure

Now you are ready to read a book! What can you tell about this book?

> What is a spy?
> Who is Simon?
> Is this a sad story or a happy one?

Learning More New Words from Your Pleasure Reading Book

After you read, write the new words in your notebook. (See page 103.) Write the word and write the sentence (or sentences) around the word. Next write the meaning (in English or your language). Then check the meaning with your teacher or in the dictionary.

Example:

Simon Simple is at the station. He is going on a train. There are policemen at the station. There are policemen on the trains. They are all working very hard. "Why are the police here?" Simon asks a man. "Look," the man says. Simon looks at the man's newspaper. *'Do you know this man?'* he reads. *'He's a **spy**! Find him! Stop him! Catch him!'*

a. New word: ____station____

b. Sentences: ____Simple Simon is at the station. He is going____ ____on a train.____

c. Meaning: ____a place to get on a train____

d. Check the meaning with your teacher or in the dictionary. Is it correct? ____yes____

Looking for a Pleasure Reading Book

Now you can look for a book to read. It must be interesting to you! It must not be very easy for you, and it must not be very difficult.

How to find the right book for you:

1. Look at the front and the back of the book.

2. Read the title (name) of the book. What is it about? Is it interesting?

3. Read the first page.

How many words are new for you? _____

      no new words → This book may be too easy for you.

      1-5 new words → This book is right for you.

      6 or more new words → This book is difficult for you.

Talking about Pleasure Reading Books

After you read a book, talk about it. Talk to your friends and to your teacher. Here are some questions to ask and answer about books:

What is the book about?

Who is the author (writer)?

Who is in the story?

Where are they?

Do you like this book? Why or why not?

Pleasure Reading Book List

➤ *Make a list of your pleasure reading books here. When you write the title of a book, put a line under it.*

1. Title _____

Author _____

Number of pages _____ Date begun _____ Date finished _____

2. Title _____

Author _____

Number of pages _____ Date begun _____ Date finished _____

3. Title _____

Author _____

Number of pages _____ Date begun _____ Date finished _____

4. Title _____

Author _____

Number of pages _____ Date begun _____ Date finished _____

5. Title _____

Author _____

Number of pages _____ Date begun _____ Date finished _____

Writing about Pleasure Reading Books

You can write about a book in a letter. Here is a letter about *Simon and the Spy*.

Dear __Maria__ ,

    I just read a book. I want to tell you about it. The book's title is __Simon and the Spy__ . The author's name is __Elizabeth Laird__ .

    This book is about __Simon and Samantha and how they__ __meet a spy on a train and then on a boat__ .

    The story is __very funny__ . The book is __easy__ to read.

    I __like__ this book __very much__ because __I like the__ __ending__ . I think you __should read it__ .

                    Your friend,

                    __Wang__

➤ *Now you write a letter about your pleasure reading book.*

Dear _____ ,

    I just read a book. I want to tell you about it. The book's title is

_____ .

The author's name is _____ .

    This book is about _____

_____ .

    The story is _____ .

The book is _____ to read.

    I _____ this book _____ because

_____ .

    I think you _____ .

                    Your friend,

                    _____

Pleasure Reading Report

➤ *Write a report about your pleasure reading book. Write the report on a piece of paper. Then give it to your teacher.*

Title of book: _____

Name of author: _____

How many pages in the book? _____

What is this book about? _____

_____

_____

Is this book true? _____ Is it easy to read? _____

Do you like this book? _____ Why? _____

_____

_____

Is this a good book for a friend to read? _____

Why? _____

_____

Part Two

Comprehension
Skills

Scanning for Key Words

What is scanning? It is a way to read very fast. You do not read all the words. You read only the words you are looking for.

In these exercises you learn to find words quickly. Then you can read quickly. Circle the key word every time you see it in the line.

Example:

Key words

1. **read**   real   (read)   reel   raid   (read)

2. **three**   tree   there   (three)   these   trees

Exercise 1

➤ *Circle the key word every time you see it in the line. Work quickly.*

Key words

1. **into**	onto	unto	into	intro	into
2. **been**	been	bean	born	been	barn
3. **back**	black	bark	back	bank	book
4. **must**	much	must	mist	mush	muse
5. **then**	them	then	ten	than	then
6. **way**	way	why	wax	way	wry
7. **out**	our	cut	oust	own	out
8. **all**	ail	all	awl	owe	alm
9. **with**	witch	with	wish	will	wilt
10. **over**	ever	aver	over	our	over

Exercise 2

➤ *Circle the key word every time you see it in the line. Work quickly.*

Key words

1. **they**	thy	they	then	them	they
2. **what**	what	when	white	what	whit
3. **down**	dawn	darn	done	dean	down
4. **may**	my	may	many	way	marry
5. **time**	twine	tine	turn	time	time
6. **would**	want	would	walked	should	world
7. **you**	you	yes	yon	you	yore
8. **also**	alas	alto	also	ails	also
9. **much**	must	mast	mush	much	munch
10. **after**	alter	alter	after	afar	otter

Exercise 3

➤ *Circle the key word every time you see it in the line. Work quickly.*

Key words

1. **before**	baffle	belief	befriend	before	belfry
2. **which**	witch	which	winch	whisk	which
3. **was**	watt	war	was	wan	wan
4. **are**	art	arc	air	ago	are
5. **were**	were	wear	were	ware	wore
6. **about**	abound	abuse	about	abut	about
7. **there**	there	their	these	theme	three
8. **new**	now	net	non	new	not

(continued on next page)

| 9. **our** | out | our | own | our | oar |
| 10. **any** | ant | nay | awry | and | any |

Exercise 4

> *Circle the key word every time you see it in the line. Work quickly.*
> **Key words**

1. **will**	wilt	wall	with	will	wild
2. **made**	made	made	make	maid	mode
3. **their**	there	these	three	their	thine
4. **years**	yours	years	yarns	years	yards
5. **did**	did	die	dill	dud	dad
6. **him**	hum	him	him	ham	hun
7. **most**	moat	must	mast	mouth	most
8. **could**	cold	culled	could	called	could
9. **your**	year	your	your	yarn	yore
10. **through**	thought	though	threw	through	tough

Exercise 5

> *Circle the key word every time you see it in the line. Work quickly.*
> **Key words**

1. **can**	car	cad	con	can	can
2. **two**	tow	too	to	two	too
3. **have**	hare	hove	have	hive	have
4. **from**	from	form	from	farm	firm
5. **not**	not	net	nut	mat	met
6. **had**	hid	had	has	has	had
7. **more**	more	mare	mere	more	mire

8. **some**	sons	soon	some	soar	soon
9. **these**	these	three	there	their	those
10. **where**	were	where	when	where	whose
11. **for**	far	fir	fur	four	for
12. **way**	why	way	wag	way	war
13. **well**	wall	wall	well	will	welt
14. **only**	any	ugly	angle	only	onto
15. **other**	antler	other	otter	odder	udder
16. **first**	forth	fist	first	first	forest
17. **such**	sick	such	sock	much	such
18. **said**	said	sail	sad	said	sale

Exercise 6

➤ *Circle the key word every time you see it in the line. Work quickly.*
Key words

1. **into**	onto	unto	into	intro	into
2. **been**	been	bean	born	bane	been
3. **back**	black	bark	back	back	book
4. **must**	much	must	mist	must	muse
5. **then**	them	then	then	than	then
6. **way**	way	why	wax	way	wry
7. **also**	alas	alto	also	ails	also
8. **much**	mulch	mast	mush	munch	much
9. **after**	alter	altar	afar	otter	after
10. **before**	baffle	belief	before	bereft	bored

(continued on next page)

11. **down**	dawn	darn	done	down	dean
12. **which**	witch	which	winch	whisk	which
13. **was**	watt	war	was	wan	wan
14. **are**	art	arc	air	ago	are
15. **were**	were	wear	ware	wore	were
16. **about**	abound	abuse	about	abut	about
17. **our**	out	our	own	our	oar
18. **any**	ant	nay	awry	and	any

Exercise 7

➤ *Circle the key word every time you see it in the line. Work quickly.*
Key words

1. **have**	hare	hove	have	hive	have
2. **from**	from	form	farm	firm	from
3. **not**	not	net	nut	mat	met
4. **their**	there	these	three	their	there
5. **more**	more	mare	mere	more	mire
6. **some**	sons	soon	some	soar	soon
7. **these**	these	three	there	their	those
8. **where**	were	where	when	where	whose
9. **time**	twine	tine	turn	time	time
10. **would**	want	would	could	should	world
11. **you**	you	yes	yon	you	yore
12. **also**	alas	alto	also	ails	also
13. **much**	must	mast	mush	much	munch
14. **after**	alter	altar	afar	otter	after

15. **from**	from	form	farm	firm	from
16. **not**	not	net	nut	mat	met
17. **had**	hid	hub	has	hat	had
18. **more**	more	mare	mere	more	mire

Exercise 8

➤ *Circle the key word every time you see it in the line. Work quickly.*

Key words

1. **always**	away	aways	always	asleep	always
2. **close**	clothes	close	class	clock	class
3. **fast**	fast	food	fist	fast	first
4. **grass**	gram	grass	gray	green	grass
5. **head**	hear	help	hair	here	head
6. **letter**	lesson	light	listen	letter	liter
7. **month**	many	month	mouth	money	morning
8. **near**	never	name	north	near	nose
9. **oil**	old	our	oil	one	all
10. **over**	oven	out	over	open	over
11. **ship**	self	she	shape	ship	sits
12. **says**	said	says	saying	sails	self
13. **read**	raid	red	ready	read	rain
14. **speak**	spoon	sleep	asleep	speak	street
15. **talk**	tall	tell	taxi	take	talk
16. **their**	there	them	their	then	their
17. **thanks**	thinks	thanks	thank	think	tanks
18. **story**	stony	store	story	stop	store

Scanning for Information

Readers often scan for information. They do not read all the words. They read only the words they need. You can learn to scan for information in these exercises. Work quickly. Remember—you do not have to read all the words!

Exercise 1

Here is a newspaper ad for some pop music concerts.

➤ **A. Scan the ad and answer the questions. Work quickly.**

1. Can you see Jimmy Buffet in July? _____

2. When can you see Meatloaf? _____

3. Which concert can you hear on August 26? _____

4. How many concerts are in July? _____

5. Who is the star on July 29? _____

6. What time is the Lynyrd Skynyrd concert? _____

7. How much are the tickets for James Taylor? _____

8. When can you see Rod Stewart? _____

➤ **B. Talk about the ads with another student.**

1. Do you like music? What kind?

2. Do you know any of the stars in this ad? Which ones?

3. Which star do you like? Why?

Exercise 2

These classified ads are not for stores or companies. People put classified ads in the newspaper. There are many things to buy and sell in these ads. Some ads are about something lost or found. Other ads tell about classes.

➤ *A. Scan the ads and answer the questions. Work quickly.*

1. How many bicycles are for sale? _____

2. What is the price of the 21" TV and VCR? _____

3. How many dogs were found? _____

4. Were any cats found? _____

5. Where was the camera lost? _____

6. What is the price of English lessons in your home? _____

7. What is the telephone number for Chinese lessons? _____

8. When does the new class for singing lessons begin? _____

9. How much is the reward for the lost keys? _____

10. Where was the piano made? _____

➤ *B. Talk about the ads with another student.*

1. Are any of these ads interesting to you? Why?

2. Look at the "Lost and Found" ads. There are two ads about cats. What do you think?

3. Can you give lessons in a language? Or a sport? Or music? Tell what you can do.

Los Angeles News

Classified Ads

For Sale	Lost and Found	Classes and Tutoring
Bed. $150. Like new. 223-3222	Lost. Keys on ring. Near High St. $25. reward. Call 321-1212.	Learn to sing. New class begins in June. Five students in a class. Ten weeks, $75. Call today! 525-0800
Table and 4 chairs. Beautiful, old. $700. 342-9982	Lost: Black and white cat. 2 years old. Near Green St. Please call 939-9310.	Math lessons. Tutor can help you! $15/hour. Call 566-7878.
Bicycle. 1 year old. 21 speeds. $75. 663-9280	Lost. Sunglasses in red case. Near School St. Reward. 773-7219	English lessons in your home. Very good teacher. $20/hour. 793-7287
Bicycle. Men's. Good for hills. $90. 641-2398	Found. Black and white cat. Green St. at City Park. 794-4582	Learn to speak Chinese. Hong Kong teacher. $25/hour. 356-4678
Piano. Made in Germany. Like new. $3,000. 663-2929	Found. Big black dog. Small ears. Short hair. Near Flower St. 393-1974	Piano lessons. Teacher from Russia. Call today. 894-0759
21" TV and VCR. 2 years old. Must sell now. $350. 769-5055	Lost. Near University Rd. Camera in brown case. Need for my job. Reward. Please call 723-2901.	English classes for beginners. Six students in a class. 736-2984

Exercise 3

Newspapers often have large ads for supermarkets.

➤ **A. Scan this supermarket ad and answer the questions. Work quickly.**

1. How much is the Oriental soup mix? _____

2. Can you find any cat food? _____

3. What kind of fruit drink is on sale? _____

4. How much is the cough syrup? _____

5. How many ounces (oz.) is the ketchup? _____

6. Can you find any milk? _____

7. What is there for babies? _____

8. How many things cost a dollar or more? _____

9. How many drinks are there? _____

10. How many ice-cream bars are in a box? _____

➤ **B. Talk about the ad with another student.**

1. You are going to this supermarket. Which things do you want to buy? Why?

2. Can you find these things in other countries?

Half Gallon•Chilled
Fruit Drinks
.58

1.17-1.66 oz.
Oriental Soup Mix
.89

28 oz.
Squeeze Ketchup
1³⁹

13 oz.
Cat Food
2/$1

4 ct.•Ice Cream Sandwiches or
Ice Cream Bars
1⁹⁹

250 ct.
Decorative Napkins
1³⁹

12 oz.
Delux Cheese Slices
1⁹⁹

Quart
Baby Juice
1⁶⁹

28 oz.•Original
Kitchen Ready Tomatoes
.79

1 lb.
Graham Crackers
1⁹⁹

4 oz.
Cough Syrup
3⁷⁹

18 oz.
Crisp Cereal
2³⁹

53

Exercise 4

Here is the table of contents of the book *Making Business Decisions*. What can you learn about this book?

➤ **A. Scan the table of contents and answer the questions. Work quickly.**

1. How many units are there? __10__

2. Which units are about food companies? _____

3. Which unit is about the clothing business? _____

4. Which company makes ice cream? _____

5. On what page does the unit about supermarkets begin? _____

6. Which units have a writing exercise about "business letters?"

_____

7. Which units are about international business or trade?

_____

8. Which unit is about new products? _____

➤ **B. Talk about the contents of this book with another student.**

1. Do you know the companies in the units? Which ones?

2. Is this an interesting book? Why or why not?

CONTENTS

To the Teacher vii

Making Inferences

What is an inference? It's a way of guessing. When you make an inference, you have some information and you guess more things from that information.

You often make inferences in your life. You can make inferences on the bus, for example. You hear two people talking. You do not know what they are talking about. But after you listen a little, you can guess what they are talking about.

Making inferences is important when you read. It can often help you understand what you are reading. Good readers, in fact, make inferences all the time. In these exercises, you can learn to make inferences.

Example:

➤ *Look at the picture and answer the questions. You must make inferences from the picture! Work with another student.*

1. Where are these people? <u>in an airplane</u>

2. What are their jobs? <u>They're both business people.</u>

3. What are they doing? <u>The man is showing something</u>
   <u>to the woman.</u>

4. What are they saying? <u>The man is saying, "Here is a</u>
   <u>photo of my family."</u>

Exercise 1

➤ *Make inferences from this picture and answer the questions. Work with another student.*

1. Where are these people? _____

_____

2. What are their jobs? _____

_____

3. What are they doing? _____

_____

4. What are they saying? _____

_____

Talk to some other students. Do they have the same answers?

Exercise 2

➤ *Make inferences from this picture and answer the questions. Work with another student.*

1. Where are these people? _____

_____

2. What are their jobs? _____

_____

3. What are they doing? _____

_____

4. What are they saying? _____

_____

Talk to some other students. Do they have the same answers?

Exercise 3

➤ *Here are some riddles about food. In riddles you must make inferences. Can you answer the questions?*

1. It's brown.
   You can drink it.
   You can put milk or sugar in it.
   It isn't tea.

   What is it? _coffee_____

2. First it's red.
   After you cook it, it's brown.

   What is it? _____

3. It's orange.
   It's often long and thin.
   Sometimes you cook it and sometimes you don't.

   What is it? _____

4. It's white.
   It's sweet.
   You can put it in coffee or tea.
   You often put it in cakes.

   What is it? _____

5. It's white.
   It's not sweet.
   You can put it on meat or vegetables.
   You don't put it in coffee.

   What is it? _____

6. It's white or brown.
   You can make sandwiches with it.
   You can put butter on it.
   You can eat it alone.

   What is it? _____

7. It can be red, green, or yellow.
   It comes from a tree.
   You can eat it anytime.
   You can cook it, too.

   What is it? _____

8. It's white.
   You must cook it.
   You can put butter on it.
   You can eat it with meat or vegetables.

   What is it?_____

Talk to another student. Do you have the same answers?

Exercise 4

➤ *Here are some riddles about places. Can you answer the questions?*

1. It's a building.
   It's for children.
   Some adults are there, too.
   The children are studying.
   The adults are teaching.

   What is it? _____

2. It's in a building.
   There are lots of tables.
   Some people are eating.
   Some people are cooking.
   Some people are bringing food to the tables.

   What is it?_____

3. It's not in a building.
   It has trees and it sometimes has flowers.
   Children like to play there.
   Dogs like to run there.
   People like to sit there.

   What is it? _____

4. It's in a building.
   People sit and work there.
   Other people stand and wait.
   Some want to get money.
   Some want to give money.

   What is it? _____

5. It's outside in the yard.
   It's small.
   It has a door but no windows.
   Something lives there.
   Cats do not like to go near it.

   What is it? _____

Talk to another student. Do you have the same answers?

Exercise 5

➤ *Here are some riddles about jobs. Can you answer the questions?*

1. He sees lots of children.
   Some children are sick.
   He helps them get well.
   He listens to the mothers and fathers.
   He tells them what to do.

   What is his job? _____

2. Sometimes she sits at a desk.
   Sometimes she walks through the store.
   She answers some people's questions.
   She helps other people at work.
   She wants lots of people in the store.

   What is her job? _____

3. He works in a tall building.
   His office is on top.
   He has meetings in restaurants.
   He makes telephone calls in his car.
   He has an airplane, too.

   What is his job?_____

4. She goes to different places around the world.
   Sometimes there are wars. Sometimes people are dying.
   She talks to the people in these places.
   Then she tells their stories to the people at home.
   Many people watch her in the evening.

   What is her job? _____

5. She sits down all day.
   But she moves around the city.
   She goes to the same places every day.
   She sees many different people.
   They pay to go with her.

   What is her job? _____

Talk to another student. Do you have the same answers?

Exercise 6

➤ *Make inferences from this part of a story. Read and answer the questions.*

The sun is going down. Jonas cannot find the road. He listens to the river and stays near it.

What is that? Jonas hears something. He listens. A man is near. A man is calling. A man wants help!

"Where are you?" Jonas calls.

"Here! Come here! Help me!" the man answers.

Jonas looks behind a big stone. "Harry!" he says. "What are you doing here?"

"I'm running from Bernie and Pete," Harry says. "But my leg is bad. I can't go on. Bernie and Pete are looking for me. They're angry. There isn't any gold in this river."

"What?" Jonas says. "But you . . . in the bar . . ."

"It's not in the water," Harry says. "It's here. Look." He brings out the bags of gold.

1. Where are these people? _____

2. What is Harry doing? _____

3. Why are Bernie and Pete angry? _____

4. What did Harry say in the bar? _____

Talk to another student. Do you have the same answers?

Exercise 7

➤ *Make inferences from this part of the story. Read and answer the questions.*

Four days later, Jenny and Blue Sky are making the beds. Suddenly they hear something. Two men are shouting. Jenny looks out of the window. She can see Jack Crane and her father in front of the farmhouse. Jack Crane's face is very red.

"*Do* it!" he shouts.

"No, I'm not going to," Sam shouts back. "It's Sunday and I don't work on Sundays. *You* do it!"

Jenny runs downstairs and out of the house. There is a strong wind and it is raining.

"What's happening?" she asks her father.

"We're leaving in the morning," Sam answers. He is walking very fast. Jenny looks at him.

"But . . . how are we going to *eat*? We don't have any money."

Sam does not answer. His eyes are cold and hard.

1. Where are these people? _____

2. What does Jack Crane want? _____

3. Why are Sam's eyes cold and hard? _____

_____

4. What does Jenny think? _____

_____

Talk to another student. Do you have the same answers?

Exercise 8

➤ *Make inferences from this part of a story. Read and answer the questions.*

Leaping Larry says, "We want to see the island."

"All right," says Duncan. "We can go in my boat."

Duncan, Larry, and Roxanne get into Duncan's boat. Jock jumps in, too. Roxanne is carrying Bobo.

Duncan takes them around the island. The sun is shining and it's a beautiful day. But Roxanne isn't happy.

"What do you do all day?" she asks Duncan.

"Well," says Duncan, "I go for walks and I fish. And sometimes I go swimming."

"Is that all?" Roxanne asks.

"Well," says Duncan, "I'm also writing a book."

"A book!" says Roxanne. "What about?"

"About Lana," says Duncan.

"Oh," says Roxanne. "That isn't very exciting."

"Listen, honey," says Larry. "We can make the island exciting. We can have pop concerts here. It's just fine for concerts. Hundreds of people can come!"

Duncan looks at Jock. Jock looks at Duncan.

"Pop concerts!" they think. "Oh, no!"

1. Where are these people? _____

2. Where does Duncan live? _____

3. Does Larry like the island? Why or why not? _____

_____

4. What does Duncan think? _____

_____

Talk to another student. Do you have the same answers?

Unit 4

Looking for Topics

What is a "topic"? A topic tells what something is about.

Good readers always look for the topic when they read. Then they can understand and remember what they read.

There are two kinds of topics. One kind of topic is the name of a group of things. Another kind of topic is the name of a thing with many parts.

Topics That Are Names of Groups

Exercise 1

➤ *What is the topic of these pictures?*

1. Topic: __birds__

2. Topic: _____

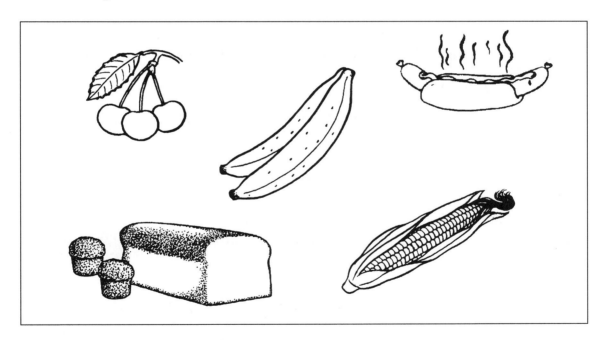

3. Topic: _____

Exercise 2

➤ *Find the topic word in each group of words and circle it. Then write the topic on the line. Work with another student.*

1. Topic: _color_

   red   yellow   blue   orange   brown   (color)

2. Topic: _____

   pop   music   rock   country   classical   jazz

3. Topic: _____

   animals   cats   dogs   horses   pigs   elephants

4. Topic: _____

   brother   son   father   men   grandfather   uncle

5. Topic: _____

   apple   banana   orange   fruit   pear   mango

6. Topic: _____

   morning   night   times of day   evening   afternoon

7. Topic: _____

   walks   talks   sleeps   builds   verbs   begins

8. Topic: _____

   shirts   clothes   dresses   pants   coats   socks

9. Topic: _____

   hotels   hospitals   banks   schools   buildings   theaters

10. Topic: _____

    Japan   Brazil   China   France   Korea   countries

Exercise 3

➤ *Find the topic word in each group of words and circle it. Then write it on the line. Work with another student.*

1. Topic: _____

    breakfast   dinner   supper   meals   lunch   snack

2. Topic: _____

    aunt   sister   women   mother   girlfriend   daughter

3. Topic: _____

    books   magazines   newspapers   letters   reading material

4. Topic: _____

    soda   coffee   orange juice   drinks   tea   water

5. Topic: _____

    teacher   doctor   taxi driver   jobs   lawyer   singer

6. Topic: _____

    table   furniture   chair   sofa   desk   bed

7. Topic: _____

    bus   car   plane   taxi   transportation   train

8. Topic: _____

    fork   spoon   knife   cup   tableware   bowl

9. Topic: _____

    basketball   football   sports   tennis   baseball

10. Topic: _____

    dining room   restaurant   coffee shop   cafe   eating places

Topics That Name Things with Many Parts

Exercise 4

➤ *These things are all part of something. What is it?*

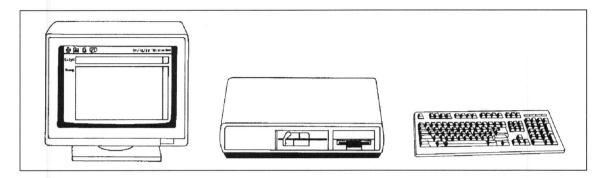

1. Topic: <u>*computer*</u>

2. Topic: _____

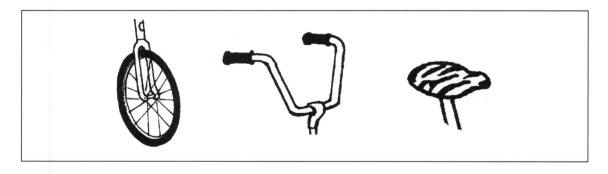

3. Topic: _____

Exercise 5

➤ *Find the topic word in each group of words and circle it. Then write it on the line. Work with another student.*

1. Topic: _____

   husband   family   son   daughter   cousin   wife

2. Topic: _____

   trees   flowers   grass   birds   bushes   garden

3. Topic: _____

   arms   legs   neck   body   head   feet

4. Topic: _____

   students   books   teacher   pens   paper   classroom

5. Topic: _____

   nose   head   mouth   ears   hair   eyes

6. Topic: _____

   wheels   doors   windows   seats   car   engine

7. Topic _____

   minute   second   hour   day   time   week

8. Topic _____

   building   roof   walls   doors   stairs   windows

9. Topic: _____

   apartment   bedroom   living room   kitchen   bathroom   hall

10. Topic: _____

    desk   computer   bookcase   office   chair   telephone

More Practice with Topics

In exercises 6-10, you can find both kinds of topics: Some topics are names of a group. Other topics are parts of something.

Exercise 6

➤ *Find a topic for each group of words. Write it on the line.*

Topics

people who work with money	people who work outside
people who work with people	people who work with their hands
people who work in government	
	people who work in a hospital
people who often work at night	people who make music

1. Topic: *people who work in government*

   mayor   president   governor   prime minister   commissioner

2. Topic: _____

   taxi driver   doctor   baker   police officer   telephone operator

3. Topic: _____

   doctor   orderly   nurse   technician   surgeon

4. Topic: _____

   cellist   pianist   violinist   trumpeter   soprano

5. Topic: _____

   teacher   doctor   nurse   lawyer   professor

6. Topic: _____

   artist   gardener   cook   nurse   pianist   surgeon

7. Topic: _____

   banker   cashier   accountant   gambler   economist

8. Topic: _____

   gardener   taxi driver   policeofficer   farmer   road worker

Exercise 7

➤ **1. This group of words has two topics. Write the topics and write the words under them. Work with another student.**

candy	orange	mango	apple	cookies
cake	chocolate	ice cream	banana	grapefruit

Topic 1: _fruit_   Topic 2: _____

_____orange_____   _____

_____   _____

_____   _____

_____   _____

_____   _____

➤ **2. This group of words also has two topics. Write the two topics and write the words under them.**

chapter	adjective	page	table of contents	paragraph
noun	pronoun	adverb	verb	title

Topic 1: _____   Topic 2: _____

_____   _____

_____   _____

_____   _____

_____   _____

_____   _____

➤ **3. Now you think of the words for these topics.**

Topic 1: _favorite foods_   Topic 2: _beautiful cities_

_____   _____

_____   _____

_____   _____

_____   _____

Look at some of your classmates' words. Do you have any of the same words? Do you have any different words?

Exercise 8

➤ *Think of a topic for each group of words and write it on the line. Then think of one more word for each topic and write it. Work with another student.*

1. Topic: _park_

   trees   bushes   birds   grass   fountain   _flowers_

2. Topic: _____

   nose   ears   mouth   hair   forehead   _____

3. Topic: _____

   meat   cheese   fruit   bread   vegetables   _____

4. Topic: _____

   car   bus   boat   train   bicycle   _____

5. Topic: _____

   soda   tea   milk   coffee   water   _____

6. Topic: _____

   uncle   brother   father   grandfather   grandson   _____

7. Topic: _____

   morning   evening   midnight   night   _____

8. Topic: _____

   book   magazine   story   poem   _____

9. Topic: _____

   three   nine   fifteen   twenty-one   _____

10. Topic: _____

    feet   legs   arms   head   neck   _____

Exercise 9

➤ *Write the topic. One word does not belong to the topic. Cross out that word. Work with another student.*

1. Topic: ___head___

   nose   ears   eyes   mouth   ~~hand~~

2. Topic: _____

   bedroom   living room   kitchen   wall   bathroom

3. Topic: _____

   England   New York   France   Mexico   China

4. Topic: _____

   hockey   baseball   basketball   football   tennis

5. Topic: _____

   runs   cries   laughs   days   talks

6. Topic: _____

   new   beautiful   clean   garden   happy

7. Topic: _____

   wheels   windows   doors   desk   engine

8. Topic: _____

   city   hour   day   week   month

9. Topic: _____

   music   food   dancing   read   drinks

10. Topic: _____

   Canada   Los Angeles   Boston   New York   Chicago

Exercise 10

➤ *Write the topic. Cross out the word that does not belong. Work with another student.*

1. Topic: _____

   juice   tea   bread   coffee   water

2. Topic: _____

   plane   bus   bicycle   boat   house

3. Topic: _____

   coat   hat   dress   clock   shirt

4. Topic: _____

   flowers   grass   desk   bush   trees

5. Topic: _____

   sister   aunt   mother   grandfather   daughter

6. Topic: _____

   arms   legs   shoes   feet   hands

7. Topic: _____

   twenty   fifteen   seventeen   thirty   ten

8. Topic: _____

   Japan   China   Vietnam   England   Korea

9. Topic: _____

   lions   panthers   elephants   tigers   dogs

10. Topic: _____

    salad   rice   banana   ice cream   spoon

Understanding and Building Sentences

When you read English, you must understand English sentences. You can learn how to find the important parts of sentences. You can also learn the right word order. These exercises can help you read English sentences.

Exercise 1

➤ **Make sentences. Draw a line from A to B.**

A	B
1. She's cooking	a bus.
2. She's drinking	in a chair.
3. He's reading	fish.
4. He's sitting	by the door.
5. She's standing	a book.
6. He's driving	coffee.

➤ **Write the sentences here.**

1. _____She's cooking fish._____

2. _____

3. _____

4. _____

5. _____

6. _____

Talk to another student about his or her sentences and your sentences. Are they the same?

Exercise 2

➤ *Make sentences. Draw a line from A to B.*

A	B
1. The dogs are eating	questions.
2. The students are asking	the windows.
3. The children are building	new clothes.
4. My friends are buying	their food.
5. Tom and Frank are closing	their father.
6. The girls are coming	their money.
7. The women are getting	to play ball.
8. The boys are helping	a doghouse.

➤ *Write the sentences here.*

1. _____

2. _____

3. _____

4. _____

5. _____

6. _____

7. _____

8. _____

Talk to another student about his or her sentences and your sentences. Are they the same?

Exercise 3

Write adjectives in the right places in these sentences. They must still be good sentences! Then write the new sentence.

Here are some adjectives. You can also use other adjectives.

young	beautiful	cold	slow	green
new	angry	hot	fast	white
old	happy	dry	tall	brown
bad	big	sick	red	yellow
good	small	sad	blue	black

1. The ___young___ man is driving a ___green___ car.

   The young man is driving a green car.

2. The _____ girl is eating a _____ sandwich.

   _____

3. A _____ cat sees a _____ dog.

   _____

4. A _____ bird lives in that _____ tree.

   _____

5. The _____ teacher is talking to a _____ girl.

   _____

6. This _____ book is about _____ cities.

   _____

7. _____ children do not like _____ animals.

   _____

8. The _____ woman is giving a _____ flower to a

   _____ man.

   _____

Talk to another student about his or her sentences and your sentences. Are they the same?

Exercise 4

➤ **A. Make sentences. Draw a line from A to B. Then put adjectives in the sentences.**

A	B
1. The horse	are talking to the _____ teacher.
2. That house	is eating a ___*big*___ apple.
3. My sister	cook _____ dinners on Saturday evenings.
4. Simon's brother	has _____ windows.
5. Some restaurants	has _____ friends.
6. The students	is flying through a _____ cloud.
7. The airplane	have _____ flowers on the tables.
8. Mr. and Mrs. Jenkins	doesn't like _____ dresses.

➤ *Write the sentences here.*

1. ___The horse is eating a big apple._____

2. _____

3. _____

4. _____

5. _____

6. _____

7. _____

8. _____

➤ **B. Write some new sentences. Put an adjective in every sentence.**

1. The horse _____

2. That house _____

3. My sister _____

4. Simon's brother _____

5. Some restaurants _____

6. The students _____

7. The airplane _____

8. Mr. and Mrs. Jenkins _____

Talk to another student about his or her sentences and your sentences in A and B. Are they the same?

Exercise 5

➤ *Write adverbs in these sentences. Then write the sentences. Here are some adverbs:*

always	sometimes	fast	well	often
never	usually	slowly	badly	quickly

1. I ___often___ read the newspaper in the morning.

   ___I often read the newspaper in the morning.___

2. I read English _____.

   _____

3. My family _____ goes to restaurants.

   _____

4. My father _____ washes the windows.

   _____

5. I do my homework _____.

   _____

6. My friend rides a bicycle _____.

   _____

7. I _____ go to the bank on Saturday.

   _____

8. My mother drives a car _____.

   _____

Talk to another student about his or her sentences and your sentences. Are they the same?

Exercise 6

➤ **A. Make sentences. Draw a line from A to B to C.**

A	B	C
1. A tall man	is learning	at night.
2. That old dog	is waiting	for you.
3. Our morning class	wakes up often	the cat's food.
4. My baby sister	is walking fast	to read well in English.
5. The new doctor	always eats	down the street.

➤ **Write the sentences here.**

1.   A tall man is walking fast down the street.

2. _____

3. _____

4. _____

5. _____

➤ **B. Write some new sentences.**

1. A tall man _____

2. That old dog _____

3. Our morning class _____

4. My baby sister _____

5. The new doctor _____

Talk to another student about his or her sentences and your sentences in A and B. Are they the same?

Exercise 7

➤ **A. Make sentences. Draw a line from A to B to C.**

A	B	C
1. Those girls	sometimes sleep	meat.
2. Some people	always eat	with the boys.
3. My parents	often play baseball	in that small room.
4. Those men	don't eat	much free time.
5. Three children	never have	very quickly.

➤ **Write the sentences here.**

1. _____

2. _____

3. _____

4. _____

5. _____

➤ **B. Write some new sentences. Put an adverb in every sentence.**

1. Those girls _____

2. Some people _____

3. My parents _____

4. Those men _____

5. Three children _____

Talk to another student about his or her sentences and your sentences in A and B. Are they the same?

Exercise 8

➤ **Which sentence is correct? Circle a or b.**

1. a. Asha Sachdev lives in Bombay, India.

   b. Bombay, India, lives Asha Sachdev in.

2. a. She a film star is very beautiful.

   b. She is a very beautiful film star.

3. a. Many people in India go to films.

 b. Many people go in India to films.

4. a. They all know and love her face.

 b. They all her face know and love.

5. a. Other people see on the walls her face.

 b. Other people see her face on the walls.

6. a. There are of her face big pictures all around the city.

 b. There are big pictures of her face all around the city.

7. a. Films are big business in India.

 b. Films are in India big business.

8. a. Every year the country about 900 films makes.

 b. Every year the country makes about 900 films.

9. a. These films have some sad parts and some happy parts always.

 b. These films always have some sad parts and some happy parts.

10. a. There always a beautiful is woman and a love story.

 b. There is always a beautiful woman and a love story.

Talk to another student about his or her sentences. Are they good sentences?

Exercise 9

 Write good sentences. Put a capital letter on the first word.

1. in Taichung, Taiwan

Ho Kwangliang

lives

Ho Kwangliang lives in Taichung, Taiwan.

2. the president

he is

of Ho Hung Ming Enterprises

_____

3. parts of shoes

   makes

   his company

   _____

4. buy parts of shoes

   many shoe companies

   from Ho's company

   _____

5. Ho's company

   every year

   $25 million

   makes

   _____

6. in eight buildings

   100 workers

   it has

   _____

7. in Shanghai, China

   now

   a new company

   Ho has

   _____

8. it makes

   too

   parts of shoes

   _____

Talk to another student about his or her sentences and your sentences. Are they the same?

Exercise 10

➤ *Write pronouns in the sentences. Here are some pronouns:*

Subject pronouns:	I	you	he	she	it	we	they
Object pronouns:	me	you	him	her	it	us	them
Possessive pronouns:	my	your	his	her	its	our	their

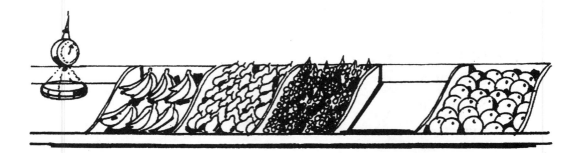

1. Mike Chi and ____his____ wife, Laura, have a fruit and vegetable store on Main Street. ____They____ work in the store with ____their____ son, Tony.

2. Tony goes to school in the morning. In the afternoon, _____ helps _____ parents in the store.

3. Mike and Laura get up very early in the morning. Mike has a big truck. He drives _____ to the city market, and _____ buys fruit and vegetables for the store.

4. Laura washes the floor and the windows of the store. She gets _____ ready for the day.

5. Many people come to the store in the morning. _____ like to buy _____ fruit and vegetables from Mike and Laura.

6. Mrs. King buys lots of oranges. _____ makes orange juice for _____ breakfast. The doctor says _____ is good for _____.

7. Manuela Garcia often buys apples. _____ likes to eat _____ for lunch at work.

8. The Chi family lives in an apartment near _____ store.

9. Laura goes home first in the afternoon. _____ goes shopping and cooks dinner.

10. At 7:00, Mike closes the store. _____ and Tony go home for dinner. After dinner, Tony does _____ homework and _____ parents watch TV.

Talk to another student about his or her sentences and your sentences. Are they the same?

Understanding Paragraphs

What is a paragraph?

A paragraph is a group of sentences about one topic. There is usually one sentence that tells you the topic. All the other sentences tell more about the topic. Good readers look for the topic that way.

1. Is this a good paragraph?

Every morning, Susan Powers eats a big breakfast. She eats two eggs, one slice of bread, and a banana. She drinks a glass of orange juice and a big cup of tea. Susan says she is ready to go to work after a good breakfast.

(Yes)   No

2. Is this a good paragraph?

Every morning, Susan Powers eats a big breakfast. She works in a bank in New York. Many people work at the bank. Some people go shopping before work. Others go shopping in the morning. On rainy days, they all bring their umbrellas to work.

Yes   (No)

Number 1 is a good paragraph. All of the sentences are about one topic: Susan's breakfast.

Number 2 is not a good paragraph. The sentences are about many different topics.

Remember

- A good paragraph has one topic.
- All the sentences are about that topic.

Exercise 1

➤ *Read about the Beatles. Think about good paragraphs.*

The Beatles

1. Can you make a good paragraph from these sentences?

    Paul McCartney is a big star in music.

    He was one of the Beatles.

    He sang many of their songs.

    Paul wrote many of the Beatles' songs.

    All around the world, people love his songs.

    ⬭Yes⬭   No

    Why? <u>All the sentences are about one topic: Paul McCartney.</u>

2. Can you make a good paragraph from these sentences?

    Ringo Starr was also a Beatle.

    He was in the Beatles group for many years.

    He sang a good song called "Yellow Submarine."

    Ringo always played the drums.

    Now he still makes music, but not with the Beatles.

    Yes   No

    Why? _____

3. Can you make a good paragraph from these sentences?

> The Beatles had four stars: John, Paul, Ringo, and George.
>
> Bruce Springsteen is also a big rock star.
>
> Some people want to be rock stars, but they can't sing.
>
> Rock music is big business.
>
> Some rock stars live in New York.

Yes   No

Why? _____

4. Can you make a good paragraph from these sentences?

> John Lennon was a Beatle, too.
>
> He wrote many of the Beatles' hit songs.
>
> He also wrote poems.
>
> He wrote songs all his life.
>
> John died in 1980.
>
> A man killed him outside his apartment building.

Yes   No

Why? _____

5. Can you make a good paragraph from these sentences?

> One person was very important to the Beatles: Brian Epstein.
>
> He did not sing or write songs.
>
> He was their business manager.
>
> He helped them get concert dates and sell records.
>
> He helped them become famous.

Yes   No

Why? _____

Exercise 2

➤ *Turn to Unit 5, Exercise 8, pages 81–82. Write the correct sentences in numbers 1 through 6 as a paragraph.*

Topic: Asha Sachdev, Indian film star

_____

_____

_____

_____

_____

_____

_____

_____

_____

_____

Exercise 3

➤ *Turn to Unit 5, Exercise 9, pages 82–83. Write sentences 1 through 8 as a paragraph.*

Topic: Ho Kwangliang's shoe companies

_____

_____

_____

_____

_____

_____

_____

_____

_____

_____

Exercise 4

➤ *Read about computers and the Internet. Ask questions: What is this paragraph about? What is the topic? Then circle the best topic for each paragraph.*

Computers and the Internet

1. Computers can do many things these days. First of all, they can add numbers fast and well. They can also print things fast and well. You can use them to send letters to people all over the world. You can find information for school or business. You can also shop for things on the computer, and you can watch a movie on the computer.

What is the best topic?

a. buying things on the computer

(b.) things you can do with a computer

c. computers

Choice a, "Buying things on the computer," is not a good topic. It tells about only part of the paragraph.

Choice b, "Things you can do with a computer," is a good topic.

Choice c, "Computers," is not a good topic. The paragraph does not tell us all about computers. It only tells about things you can do with computers. It does not tell, for example, about how to use computers.

2. Do you have an e-mail (electronic mail) address? Millions of people around the world have e-mail addresses. With e-mail, you can "talk" with people from Montevideo to Kyoto. It does not cost very much, and it is fast. E-mail helps many people with their work. Other people use e-mail for fun. They talk with their family, or they "meet" people with the same interests.

a. telephone communication

b. how e-mail helps at work

c. how people use e-mail

3. E-mail works in a very new way. You do not use the telephone, but you must have a telephone line. You write your letter on the computer. Then you tell the computer to send it to someone. Your computer sends it by telephone line to a big computer. The big computer sends your letter to another big computer. That computer sends it to the small computer on the address. That is how people use e-mail to "talk."

a. how e-mail works

b. how the Internet talks to computers

c. how a telephone line works

4. The Internet is not only e-mail. People use the Internet in other ways, too. You can use the Internet to find something in a library. The library can be in any country in the world. Your computer "talks" to the computer at the library. Then you can ask to read books or newspapers at the library. You can also ask the library to send information. The information travels by the Internet to your computer. Then you can use it whenever you want.

a. using the Internet for e-mail

b. using the library for information

c. using the library on the Internet

5. Another way to use the Internet is through the World Wide Web (WWW). On the WWW, you can find "sites." Companies, universities, and cities make these sites so you can learn about them. There are pictures and a lot of information. You can use the WWW, for example, before you travel. You ask your computer to find the site of a city. Then you can get information about that city. Or you can ask for the site of a company. You can learn about that company before you do business with them.

a. getting information about a new city

b. many ways to use the Internet

c. using WWW on the Internet

Exercise 5

➤ *Circle the best topic for each paragraph.*

A Special Sport

1. Swimming, bicycling, and running are three very popular sports. Some people like to do all three sports in one race. They can do all three in a triathlon race. *Triathlon* means "three sports." In a triathlon the people must first swim for a mile (1.6 km). Then they must ride a bicycle for about 10 miles (16 km). And then they must run for three miles (4.8 km). You must be a very strong person to win a triathlon!

a. what people do in a triathlon

b. popular sports

c. swimming in a triathlon

2. The men and women in triathlons are called triathletes. Triathletes must work hard all year to get ready. Every day, they run and swim and ride their bicycles. They must also do special exercises for their bodies. After many months of work, they are ready for a race. There are many races in many countries. One famous triathlon is the Ironman race in Hawaii. Another is the Noosa race in Australia. Triathletes come to these races from all over the world.

a. the Ironman race

b. races in many countries

c. triathletes and triathlons

3. Karen Smyers and Mark Allen are two famous triathletes. Karen Smyers, 34 years old, is from the United States. She gets ready for triathlons all year, and she goes to many races. That is her job. The Nike company gives her money to live. Mark Allen also is a full-time triathlete. He is 37 years old, and he is from the United States. In 1995, Karen and Mark were the winners in triathlons in many different countries. They also were the winners in the Ironman race in Hawaii.

a. triathletes from the United States

b. the winners of the 1995 Ironman race

c. the best triathletes of 1995

Exercise 6

➤ *There is a sentence missing from each paragraph in this exercise. The missing sentences are in the box. Write the correct sentence in each paragraph. Then write the topic.*

Writers in the English Language

1. Topic: _____

     Edna O'Brien lives in England, but she is Irish. She writes stories and books about Irish people. Some of her stories are about life in Ireland in the past and others are about Ireland today. They are always very real. _____

_____

_____. They are also very true to life— sometimes funny and sometimes sad. *The Country Girls* and *Time and Tide* are two of O'Brien's books.

2. Topic: _____

     Thomas Keneally is an Australian writer. He lives in Sydney with his family. But often he is not at home. _____

_____

_____. Keneally's most famous book is about Nazi Germany during World War II. It tells the story of about 1,000 Jewish people and a man named Schindler. Schindler helped these people live through those terrible times. Keneally went to Germany and many other countries to talk to people about Schindler. This book, *Schindler's List,* was made into a movie.

3. Topic: _____

Toni Morrison is an African-American writer. She often writes about African-American women. She tells about their lives and about the terrible things that happen to them. In Morrison's books we learn a lot about these women.

_____

_____. In 1993, Morrison won the Nobel Prize for Literature. Two of her most famous books are *Beloved* and *Jazz*.

- He writes books about different places, so he has to go to those places.
- We see through their eyes, and we learn what they are thinking and feeling.
- We can almost see the Irish countryside and hear the people speaking.

Exercise 7

➤ *A. Here are two topics. A sentence for each topic is already there. Find the other sentences for each topic in the box. Write them on the lines after the first sentence. (You can change the order later to make good paragraphs.)*

Topic 1: Drinks that are good for your health
    Some kinds of drinks are very good for your health.

_____

_____

_____

_____

_____

_____

Topic 2: Drinks that are not good for your health
    Some popular drinks are not good for your health.

_____

_____

_____

_____

_____

_____

- Milk is another healthy drink.
- Doctors say it is bad for your stomach and your head.
- Many people drink cola, but it is not good for you.
- It is very good for children and also for women.
- A little coffee is okay, but lots of coffee is bad.
- Orange juice is one of these healthy drinks.
- Some doctors think this is the way to a healthy life.
- It has lots of sugar, so it is bad for your teeth.
- So drink lots of orange juice and milk!
- Another drink that can be bad for you is coffee.
- It has lots of good things in it.
- It has other bad things in it, too.

➤ **B. Look at the sentences for each topic again. Rewrite the sentences in the right order. Make a good paragraph.**

Paragraph 1

_____
_____
_____
_____
_____
_____
_____

Paragraph 2

_____
_____
_____
_____
_____
_____
_____
_____

Exercise 8

➤ *In each paragraph there is one extra sentence. It is not about the topic. Find the sentence and cross it out. Then write the topic.*

Hobbies

1. Topic: ___Rollerblading___

Rollerblading is a very popular new sport. People in many countries around the world go rollerblading. Rollerblades go on your feet like roller skates and ice skates. They have little wheels, like roller skates. When you go rollerblading, you go very fast. You must be careful! You must not go on streets with lots of traffic or people. ~~It is also a good idea to ride your bicycle.~~ At first, you must go slowly and you must have special clothes. After you learn, you can go fast and have fun!

The sentence: "It is also a good idea to ride your bicycle" is not about rollerblading. So it is crossed out.

2. Topic: _____

In his free time, Jeff loves to go bicycling. After many hours in the office, he wants exercise. So on weekends he goes for long bicycle rides. He works just a few miles from home. Sometimes he rides for a few hours and sometimes he rides all day. Some of his friends also ride bicycles. They often ride their bicycles together. The doctor says Jeff is very healthy and has very strong legs!

3. Topic: _____

On summer days, Liz works in her garden. She has some flowers and lots of vegetables. She likes the flowers, but she doesn't work with them a lot. She works most of the time with the vegetables. Liz's husband likes going to the movies. She likes to grow vegetables, and she also likes to cook them. She does not eat meat, but she eats lots of her vegetables. Liz says they are much better than the vegetables from the store.

4. Topic: _____

Mike loves to cook. He cooks all kinds of dishes, but his favorite dishes are desserts. He says cooking is very relaxing. When he is working in the kitchen, he thinks only about cooking. He doesn't think about work or bad things. He can bake big, beautiful cakes with fruit or with chocolate. Children must not eat a lot of chocolate every day. On Saturdays, Mike has lots of time for cooking. He makes a very good dinner and a special dessert. Then he and his family have a good meal.

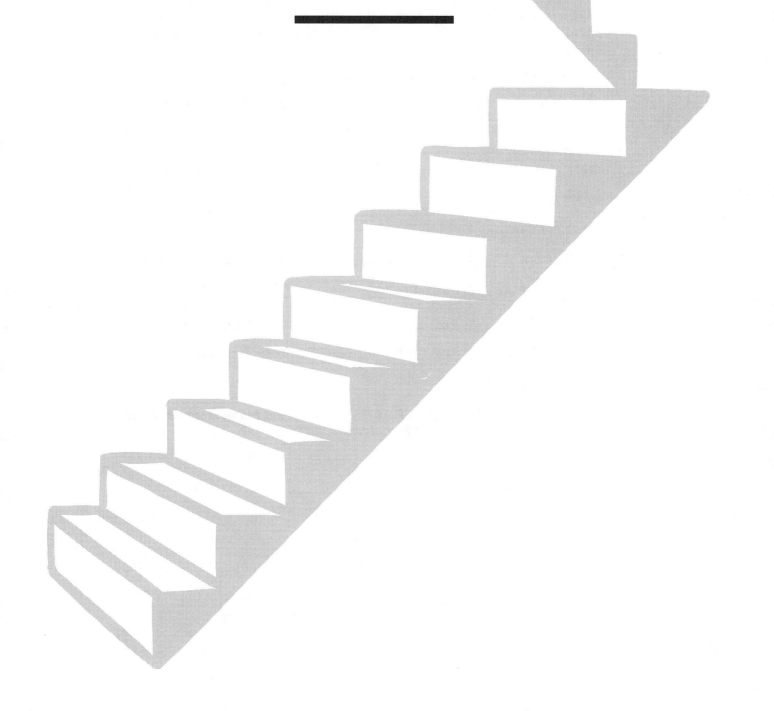

Part Three

Vocabulary Building

New Words from Your Reading

Learn new words every week. It is important to *write* new words. You can remember them much better that way. Here is a good way to learn new words:

a. Write the new word. Be sure the spelling is correct.

b. Write the sentence (or sentences) around the word from your reading.

c. Write the meaning of the new word in English or in your own language.

d. Check the meaning with your teacher or in the dictionary.

Example:

a. New word: __bridge__

b. Sentences: __They come to a river with a bridge. Some__
   __people are on the bridge.__

c. Meaning: __something that goes across a river__

d. Check the meaning with your teacher or in the dictionary.

   Is it correct? __yes__

➤ **A. Look back at the fables in Part One, Unit 1. Find ten new words. Write the words below. Follow the four steps.**

Date: _____

1. a. New word: _____

   b. Sentence(s): _____

   _____

   c. Meaning: _____

   _____

   d. Check the meaning. Is it correct? _____

2. a. New word: _____

    b. Sentence(s): _____

    _____

    c. Meaning: _____

    _____

    d. Check the meaning. Is it correct? _____

3. a. New word: _____

    b. Sentence(s): _____

    _____

    c. Meaning: _____

    _____

    d. Check the meaning. Is it correct? _____

4. a. New word: _____

    b. Sentence(s): _____

    _____

    c. Meaning: _____

    _____

    d. Check the meaning. Is it correct? _____

5. a. New word: _____

    b. Sentence(s): _____

    _____

    c. Meaning: _____

    _____

    d. Check the meaning. Is it correct? _____

6. a. New word: _____

    b. Sentence(s): _____

    _____

    c. Meaning: _____

    _____

    d. Check the meaning. Is it correct? _____

7. a. New word: _____

   b. Sentence(s): _____

     _____

   c. Meaning: _____

     _____

   d. Check the meaning. Is it correct? _____

8. a. New word: _____

   b. Sentence(s): _____

     _____

   c. Meaning: _____

     _____

   d. Check the meaning. Is it correct? _____

9. a. New word: _____

   b. Sentence(s): _____

     _____

   c. Meaning: _____

     _____

   d. Check the meaning. Is it correct? _____

10. a. New word: _____

   b. Sentence(s): _____

     _____

   c. Meaning: _____

     _____

   d. Check the meaning. Is it correct? _____

B. **Now get a small notebook for vocabulary. Every week look back at your pleasure reading. Write the new words in your notebook. First, write the date. Then write the new word, the sentence(s), and the meaning.**

New Words Quiz Do you know all your new words from last week? Write all the new words. Then write the meanings. *Do not look back!*

New Words	Meaning
1. _____	_____
	_____
2. _____	_____
	_____
3. _____	_____
	_____
4. _____	_____
	_____
5. _____	_____
	_____
6. _____	_____
	_____
7. _____	_____
	_____
8. _____	_____
	_____
9. _____	_____
	_____
10. _____	_____
	_____

Are these meanings correct? Look back at your notebook and see. Look again at the words from last week. Look at the words from the weeks before. Do you know them now? Do a New Words Quiz every week.

The 100 Words

Do you know about the "100 words"? You see these words very often when you read in English. You know many of them already. Good readers know them all very well. They read the words very quickly. They do not have to stop and think. This way, good readers can think more about the ideas. They understand better.

➤ **Now you can learn the 100 words. Here is the list of words:**

a	from	next	these
about	had	no	they
after	has	not	this
all	have	now	through
also	he	of	time
an	her	on	to
and	here	one	two
any	him	only	up
are	I	or	was
as	if	other	way
at	in	our	we
back	into	out	well
be	is	over	were
been	it	said	what
before	its	she	when
but	like	so	where
by	many	some	which
can	may	such	who
could	me	than	will
did	more	that	with
do	most	the	would
down	much	their	years
even	must	them	yes
first	my	then	you
for	new	there	your

Exercise 1

➤ *Learn to spell the 100 words. Then you can read them quickly. Write in the missing letters. Then write the word.*

1. d _o_ _do_____

2. w _ s _____

3. b _ t _____

4. t h _ _____

5. w i l _ _____

6. y o _ _____

7. w _ y _____

8. o _ t _____

9. w _ _____

10. s _ _ e _____

11. s u _ h _____

12. w _ t h _____

13. l i k _ _____

14. o n l _ _____

15. m _ n y _____

16. b _ e n _____

17. u _ _____

18. b a _ k _____

19. y o _ r _____

20. a b _ u t _____

21. w o u l _ _____

22. a _ t e r _____

23. w h e _ e _____

24. b e _ o r e _____

Exercise 2

➤ *Write in the missing letters. Then write the word.*

1. s _ _____

2. m _ r e _____

3. b e e _ _____

4. a _ l _____

5. w e r _ _____

6. t h _ m _____

7. y _ s _____

8. i _ t o _____

9. w _ r e _____

10. s _ i d _____

11. e v _ n _____

12. d _ w _ _____

13. t i m _ _____

14. o _ e r _____

15. f _ o m _____

16. m _ y _____

17. c o u _ _ _____

18. w h i c _ _____

19. y e _ r s _____

20. t h e i _ _____

21. n e x _ _____

22. t _ e s e _____

23. w h e _ _____

24. t h _ y _____

Exercise 3

➤ **Write in the missing letters. Then write the word. (Some have more than one right answer.)**

1. y o u r _____   13. t h e _____
2. w h a t _____   14. w __ __ t _____
3. h a v e _____   15. e __ __ n _____
4. n e t _____   16. m __ s t _____
5. s a i __ _____   17. w o __ __ __ _____
6. t h __ n _____   18. t __ __ m _____
7. t h __ t _____   19. o __ r _____
8. c a __ _____   20. a b __ __ t _____
9. h __ r e _____   21. s h __ _____
10. a __ y _____   22. w e __ __ _____
11. t h i __ _____   23. o __ h __ r _____
12. t __ m __ _____   24. d __ __ n _____

Exercise 4

➤ **Write in the missing letters. Then write the word. (Some have more than one right answer.)**

1. __ s _____   9. __ a y _____
2. __ i d _____   10. __ u t _____
3. __ i m _____   11. __ o w _____
4. __ o _____   12. __ y _____
5. __ e r e _____   13. __ h i c h _____
6. __ i m e _____   14. __ h e i r _____
7. __ h e n _____   15. __ t h e r _____
8. __ a n y _____   16. __ h e r e _____

Exercise 5

Some of the 100 words are in this puzzle. You can read words across (like this →) or down (like this ↓).

➤ *Find these words and circle them:*

after	are	did	had	me	of	they
all	before	down	he	most	or	to
also	but	even	him	my	our	up
and	by	for	in	new	some	way
any	can	from	may	no	then	your

```
N  A  F  T  E  R  F  R  O  M
E  L  Z  O  H  A  D  B  U  T
W  S  R  N  I  N  A  L  L  H
D  O  W  N  M  A  Y  A  R  E
I  M  O  S  T  N  O  C  A  N
D  E  V  E  N  D  U  O  F  A
B  E  F  O  R  E  R  X  T  N
L  Z  O  U  R  S  T  H  E  Y
W  L  R  P  H  A  I  M  O  O
A  N  E  R  E  L  N  E  B  Y
Y  T  O  M  Y  S  O  O  R  C
```

Exercise 6

➤ *Many of the 100 words are in this puzzle. Find 20 words and circle them.
Then write them below the puzzle.*

```
T   H   R   O   U   G   H   L   N   O
I   A   B   O   U   T   O   W   O   N
M   S   Y   O   U   H   V   H   W   I
E   V   E   N   B   E   E   E   B   Y
R   N   S   I   T   S   R   R   E   T
B   E   F   O   R   E   Z   E   I   F
A   N   Y   F   A   B   O   U   T   I
C   A   N   T   W   O   U   L   D   R
K   N   O   O   N   A   T   H   A   S
M   O   S   T   O   T   H   E   R   T
```

_____   _____

_____   _____

_____   _____

_____   _____

_____   _____

_____   _____

_____   _____

_____   _____

_____   _____

_____   _____

**Talk to another student about his or her words and your words. Are they
the same?**

Exercise 7

➤ *Some of the 100 words are in these sentences. Write in the missing letters in those words.*

1. Allen: W <u>o u l d</u> yo__ lik__ so__e milk w__ __h
   y__u__ coffee?

   Lynne: N__, thanks. __ l_k__ black coffee.

2. Suha: Wh__t __s yo__r name?
   Yuki: M__ name i__ Yuki.
   Suha: I__ th__t a Japanese name?
   Yuki: Ye__, i__ __s.

3. Pat: Whe__e a__e yo__ fr__ __?
   Stan: I'm fr__ __ Texas.
   Pat: D__ yo__ li__ __ t__ ride horses?
   Stan: N__. No__ al__ Texans li__e t__ ride horses!

4. Stefan: D__ yo__ li__ __ t__ read love stories?
   Milly: N__, I don't. I l__ __e to read ab__ __ __ __
   science an__ computers. Th__y 're m__ __h
   m__r__ interesting.

5. Craig: Wh__n di__ y__ __ call yo__r mother?
   Ivan: I called h__ __ be__ __ __ __ lunch.
   Craig: W__s sh__ a__ home?

6. Ivan: No, s__ __ w__s still __t work.
   Craig: Wh__ __ e does s__ __ work?
   Ivan: A__ __ bank i__ New York.
   Craig: Does s__ __ come b__ck home f__ __ lunch?
   Ivan: N__, s__ __ eats lunch a__ work.

Exercise 8

➤ *Read the sentences. Fill in the letters. Then write the words in the puzzle.*

Across

1. Do you have m__ book?
4. I w__ __ __d like some tea.
6. W__ have no class on Sunday.
7. Will she come b__ __ __ today?
9. He's going to Chicago n__ __ __ Tuesday.
10. Where a__ __ you from?
11. I'm n__ __ a student.
12. Ask Tom and Helen for a ride. T__ __ __ have a car.

Down

2. I want to talk to y__ __.
3. She d__ __ all the work yesterday.
5. Do you l __ __ __ orange juice?
6. W__ __ __ is the class party?
8. Sunday comes a__ __ __ __ Saturday.
10. He likes to read a__ __ __ __ cars.
13. Will you b__ home today?

Learning about Context

What is context? It is the sentence or sentences around a word. The context can tell you a lot about a word.

These exercises can help you learn about context. Some words are missing in each story. You must use the context to find the right words.

First read the story. Think about the context for each missing word. Then look for the right words.

Example:

Mara Milvaney is 36 years old. Mara and her family live in a small _____ in Australia.

What is the missing word?

horse	meat	girl	town	yard

The missing word is *town*. It is the only word that is good for this context. A family does not live in a horse, a meat, a girl, or a yard.

Exercise 1

➤ **Read the story. Write the words in the right places.**

horse	meat	girl	town	yard

Mara Milvaney is 36 years old. Mara and her family live in a small __town__ in Australia. Mara and her husband, Dan, have three children, two boys and a _____. They live in a small house with a large _____. The children like animals very much. The family has three cats, two dogs, and a _____.

Mara and Dan also like animals. They have a sheep farm. They sell the young sheep for _____. People in Europe and the United States buy the meat. Mara also sells the sheep's wool for clothes. Australian wool goes to many countries.

Exercise 2

➤ *Read the story. Write the words in the right places.*

fisherman	garden	evening	boat	sea

Malcolm Morris is 29 years old. He lives in Charlotteville, Tobago. Tobago is a small country in the Caribbean Sea. Malcolm's town is near the _____. There are few cars in this town, but there are many boats.

Malcolm is a _____. Every morning he goes out early in his _____ and gets some fish. In the afternoon he works in his vegetable _____. He eats lots of fish and vegetables. He also sells some fish in another town. In the _____ he sometimes works with the other fishermen. They often work on their boats. Sometimes he sits in a cafe with his friends. They like to talk about fishing and life.

Exercise 3

➤ **Read the story. Write the words in the right places. This time there is an extra word!**

| daughter | housework | yard | bread | friends | store |

Lidia Mazza is 89 years old. She lives in Bazzano, a small town in Italy. She lives in the same house with her daughter, her daughter's daughter, and her daughter's daughter's _____! Her son and his children live in the next town.

Mrs. Mazza does not work in the house now. Her daughter does the _____. Mrs. Mazza often works in the garden. She loves her flowers and vegetables. She also goes out to the _____ every morning. Sometimes she walks and sometimes she takes her bicycle. She buys milk and _____ for her family. She talks with the people in the store or with _____ on the street. She likes to tell them about her family.

Exercise 4

➤ **Read the story. Write the words in the right places. There is an extra word!**

planes	family	countries	company	war	soldiers

Diem Tam Tranh is 58 years old. He lives in Ho Chi Minh City, Vietnam. He and his wife have two sons. All the people in his _____ work in Tranh's company. Fourteen other people also work for Tranh. The _____ is in a small building near the city. It makes scissors.

In Vietnam, there was war for many years. Tranh was a soldier in the _____. Some of his workers were also soldiers. Tranh finds old trucks and _____ from the war. His workers take parts to the factory. They make scissors from the parts. They are very good scissors. He sells them in 14 _____ around the world.

Exercise 5

➤ *Read this story. Think of words for the spaces.*

John Utsi lives in Jokkmokk, Sweden. He is 43 years old. He is a writer for a newspaper. He also writes _____ about the Sami people. In the past, these _____ lived very far from cities. They lived in tents, and they moved the tents often. They went after reindeer. From the reindeer they had milk and _____.

John's family are Sami people. John and his wife, Elin, and their two daughters live in a city. But every year they go to Lake Kutjaure. They live in a tent for two _____. They go after reindeer. John and Elin work a lot in that time. But they like this life. And the _____ like the tents and the reindeer.

Exercise 6

➤ *Read the story. Think of words for the spaces.*

Salim Al Wahaibi is 12 years old. He lives in Al Mintirib, Oman. Oman is a small country on the Arabian Sea. Salim has a 9-year-old brother, Talib. Five days a week, Salim and Talib _____ to school.

On the weekend, their life changes. Every weekend, there are camel races near Al Mintirib. Salim's father _____ two camels. Salim and Talib get on the camels. Other boys get on other camels. Then all the camels _____ fast. Salim's father _____ a truck next to the camels. He calls to the camels, and he calls to his boys. The other fathers call to their camels and their boys. Then the race _____. But the boys can't stop the camels! The fathers must run and stop them.

Guessing
Word Meanings

Context can help you understand new words. You read the context (the sentences) around the new word. Then you make a guess about the meaning.

In these exercises, you can learn to guess from the context. When you are doing the exercises, do not use a dictionary. Do not ask your teacher or your classmates.

After you finish each exercise, you can check the meanings. Then you can use a dictionary or ask your teacher.

Example:

1. We have a little white cat. She is always hungry. We give her milk in a *bowl* on the kitchen floor. She drinks all the milk in a very short time. Then she wants more!

   What is a *bowl?* It's a large cup.

Exercise 1

➤ *Write the answers in English or in your own language. Or you can draw a picture.*

1. My friend Raymond is a very *lazy* person. He doesn't like to work. He doesn't like to play sports. He likes to sit and watch television. And he likes to sleep.

   What is a *lazy* person? _____

2. Can you see the *nest* in that tree? There are four baby birds in it. They are calling for their mother. Look! Now the mother is coming. She has some food for her babies.

   What is a *nest?* _____

3. Quick! Call the police! There is a man near my house. He has a *mask* on his face. You can see only his eyes. His clothes are all black.

   What is a *mask?* _____

(continued on next page)

4. I live in a tall building in Chicago. My home is on the sixth floor. But I don't use the *elevator* often. I don't like elevators. They are too small! They are too slow! I like to walk up to the sixth floor.

   What is an *elevator*? _____

5. The new store was often empty. This morning there was only one *customer*. She was a young woman. She wanted to buy some Levi's jeans. She didn't like the jeans in the store. So she went away.

   What is a *customer*? _____

6. There is a terrible *traffic jam* on the road to London. All the cars are stopped. You can't go left or right. You have to wait for a long time!

   What is a *traffic jam*? _____

Exercise 2

➤ *Write the answers in English or in your own language. Or you can draw a picture.*

1. These bananas are beautiful. But they are not *ripe*. They are still very green. We can't eat them today. Please put them away. We can eat them next week.

   What is *ripe* fruit? _____

2. Roger often wakes up in the night. Sometimes he wants to drink some water. But sometimes he has a *nightmare*. He sees terrible things. He hears bad things. Then he can't go back to sleep.

   What is a *nightmare*? _____

3. There is a *beggar* in front of the store. Poor woman, she doesn't have a coat. It's very cold today. She is asking people for some money. Some people give her money. Other people don't want to look at her.

   What is a *beggar*? _____

4. After all the rain, the river water was brown. It was full of *trash*. There was lots of paper. There were bags and bottles. There were old chairs and televisions.

   What is *trash*? _____

5. This is not my *glove!* It doesn't go on my hand. It's Tenko's glove. She has very small hands. But where is my glove? I can't find it! My hands are getting cold.

   What is a *glove?* _____

6. Lily wants to get a *pet.* Her mother says she can't have a dog. Lily asks, "What about a cat?" But Lily's father doesn't want a cat. "What about a bird?" Lily asks. "Okay," say her mother and father. So Lily is going to get a bird.

   What is a *pet?* _____

Exercise 3

➤ *Write the answers in English or in your language. Or you can draw a picture.*

1. We are going to England for a month. We can go to many cities and towns by train. Then we want to drive to some villages. So we want to *rent* a car. Does it cost a lot in England?

   What does *rent* mean? _____

2. Joel is reading a *poem* by Emily Dickinson. It is a very short poem—25 words. He says it is not easy to read but is very beautiful and sad.

   What is a *poem?* _____

3. My wife and I want to buy a new car, but we don't have much money. We can't ask my father for help. He doesn't have much money. We must go to the bank. They can give us a *loan.*

   What is a *loan?* _____

4. Please do not *shout!* I am not old, and my ears are still good. I am here next to you, and I can hear you very well.

   What does *shout* mean? _____

5. There is a terrible *mess* in the yard! There is paper and food on the grass. The table and chairs are on the ground. Your dog did it! I don't want your dog in my yard again!

   What is a *mess?*_____

6. Estelle's house was *huge.* It had 25 large rooms. There was also a large and beautiful garden. Some people wanted to buy the house and make a hotel. But Estelle said no. She liked her big house, and she did not want to move.

   What is a *huge* house? _____

Exercise 4

➤ *Write your answers in English or in your language. Or you can draw a picture.*

1. I am going to the *bakery* now. Do you want some bread? They make very long French bread, and it's very good. They also make very good cakes and cookies. We often get their chocolate cake.

   What is a *bakery?* _____

2. I am not going to go to that restaurant again! The food was *awful!* The pizza was black, the vegetables were old, and the coffee was terrible!

   What is *awful* food?_____

3. We must go to the animal doctor with the cat. The cat must not run and jump in the car. We must put her in a *cage.* Then we can put the cage in the car and go to the doctor.

   What is a *cage?* _____

4. Do you want to go up the mountain? You must go on that *path.* It is a small path. You can't drive the car on it. You must park the car here and walk up the path.

   What is a *path?* _____

5. Please do not *push!* You must all wait here. You must stand in line. It is still early. The film doesn't start now. It starts in 15 minutes. Then you can go in.

   What does *push* mean?_____

6. Julie is a very *smart* girl. She always has the right answers for the teacher. She does her homework fast. She never has any wrong answers in her homework. Sometimes she helps the other students.

   What is a *smart* girl? _____

Learning New Words in Categories

In Part Three, Unit 1, you learned new words from your pleasure reading. In this unit, you are going to learn new words in another way—in categories.

A category is like a topic. It tells about words that go together. It helps you remember the words.

Category: Favorite foods in the United States

steak	fried chicken
hamburgers	hot dogs
spaghetti	pizza
tacos	sandwiches
muffins	pancakes
apple pie	ice cream
brownies	chocolate chip cookies

➤ *Write the name of your country or home city in the blank. Then write some words for this category.*

Category: Favorite foods in _____

_____   _____

_____   _____

_____   _____

_____   _____

Talk to another student about his or her favorite foods.

Exercise 1

➤ *Think about your favorite place.*

My Favorite Place: <u>Yankee Stadium in New York City</u>

Some words for Yankee Stadium:

baseball	win
ticket	fans
hot dogs	radio
catch	lights

My Favorite Place: _____

Some words for my favorite place. (You can use a dictionary.)

_____   _____

_____   _____

_____   _____

_____   _____

_____   _____

Show your words to another student. Don't tell your favorite place! Can he or she guess?

Talk about your favorite place. Why do you like it? Use the words on your list.

Do you know all the words on the other student's list? Write the new words in your notebook.

Exercise 2

➤ *Think about jobs you like. Don't work with another student. Write the names of ten jobs. Use a dictionary.*

Names of Jobs

1. _____

2. _____

3. _____

4. _____

5. _____

6. _____

7. _____

8. _____

9. _____

10. _____

Talk to the students in your class. Ask each student which job he or she wants.

Write a student's name next to every job.

Look at the job list of another student. Do you know all the names of the jobs? Write the new words in your notebook.

Exercise 3

➤ *A. Look in your handbag or briefcase. Write the names of ten things you find in it. Use a dictionary. Don't work with another student.*

_____   _____

_____   _____

_____   _____

_____   _____

_____   _____

Show your list to another student and look at his or her list. Do you know all his or her words? Write the new words in your notebook.

➤ **B. Think of a famous person. Everyone in the class must know this person. It can be a film or music or sports star, a president, a writer, or an artist. What things can we find in that famous person's bag? Write ten things.**

_____	_____
_____	_____
_____	_____
_____	_____
_____	_____

Show your list to another student. Do not tell him or her the name of the person. Can he or she tell you the name?

Look at the other student's list. Who is the person for his or her list? Do you know all his or her words? Write the new words in your notebook.

Exercise 4

➤ *Which words go with village life? Which words go with city life? Some words can go with both. Write the words under a category. Don't work with another student.*

Village Life or City Life?

river	dig	dirty
bicycle	mountains	apartment
farm	park	hole
traffic	cloud	afraid
apple	newspaper	government
fly	bridge	quiet
police	mouse	noise
laugh	doorbell	chicken

Village Life   **City Life**

_____   _____

_____   _____

_____   _____

_____   _____

_____   _____

_____   _____

_____   _____

_____   _____

_____   _____

_____   _____

_____   _____

_____   _____

Write three more words for village life and three more words for city life.

_____   _____

_____   _____

_____   _____

Look at another student's list. Do you have the same words? Write the new words from his or her list in your notebook.

Exercise 5

➤ *Which things do you like doing? Which things do you not like doing? Write the words under a category. Don't work with another student.*

Things I Like Doing/Things I Don't Like Doing

dancing	cooking
eating in restaurants	fishing
walking	sleeping
drinking tea	going to the seaside
playing computer games	listening to music
running	studying English
riding a bicycle	watching television
reading the newspaper	driving a car
working with my hands	going to the movies
buying clothes	writing letters

Things I Like Doing

_____

_____

_____

_____

_____

_____

_____

_____

_____

_____

Things I Don't Like Doing

_____

_____

_____

_____

_____

_____

_____

_____

_____

_____

Look at the lists of the other students in your class. Is any list the same as yours?

Exercise 6

➤ *Make two categories. Write the categories on the lines. Then write the words under the categories. (Some words can go in both categories.)*

office	notebook	manager	pay
lunch	fax	grades	computer
lesson	teacher	telephone	clock
job	eraser	classroom	e-mail

Category: _____   Category: _____

_____   _____

_____   _____

_____   _____

_____   _____

_____   _____

_____   _____

_____   _____

Look at another student's categories and lists. Are they the same as yours?

Exercise 7

➤ *These words are in the stories in Part One of this book. Make two categories of words. Then think of names for these categories.*

1. hungry   easy   wise   terrible   alone   strong

Category: ___bad things___   Category: ___good things___

_____hungry_____   _____easy_____

_____terrible_____   _____wise_____

_____alone_____   _____strong_____

2. mouse   red   young   old   wolf   big   horse
   duck   happy   easy   sheep   strong   turtle   cat

Category: _____   Category: _____

_____   _____

_____   _____

_____   _____

_____   _____

_____   _____

_____   _____

_____   _____

Exercise 8

➤ **A. Look at the stories in Part One. Work with another student. Find 16 new words. Write the words here.**

_____   _____

_____   _____

_____   _____

_____   _____

_____   _____

_____   _____

_____   _____

_____   _____

➤ **B. Make two categories for these words. Write the names of the categories.**

Category: _____   Category: _____

_____   _____

_____   _____

_____   _____

_____   _____

_____   _____

_____   _____

Work with another pair of students. Show them your lists and look at their lists. Do you have the same categories?

Part Four

Thinking Skills

Do you think in English when you are reading? Or do you think in your language? You can understand better if you think in English. These exercises can help you learn to think in English.

➤ *Circle the best answer.*

Edwin works in a restaurant. He is the only cook. He cooks lunch and dinner. He does not cook breakfast. The restaurant is closed

    a. in the evening.   ⓒ in the morning.

    b. at lunch time.   d. on Tuesdays.

The right answer is c, "in the morning." Morning is the time for breakfast. Edwin does not cook breakfast and Edwin is the only cook. That means the restaurant is not open for breakfast. So the restaurant is closed in the morning.

Answer a, "in the evening," is not right. Breakfast is not an evening meal. Dinner is the evening meal, and Edwin cooks dinner. The restaurant is not closed in the evening.

Answer b, "at lunch time," is not right. Edwin cooks lunch, so the restaurant is not closed at lunch time.

Answer d, "on Tuesdays," is not right. The sentences do not tell about the days of the week.

Guidelines for Thinking Skills Exercises

- Do some thinking skills exercises every week.
- Work quickly and don't use a dictionary.
- Try to guess the meaning of new words.
- Think in English to find the correct answer.
- Remember: Your first guess is often the right one!

Exercise 1

➤ *Circle the best answer.*

1. Can you see that airplane? It's high in the sky. It's going far away. It's going

   a. to school.   c. to Australia.

   b. home.   d. to the country.

2. There is a big airplane from Ireland. It's coming down. Now it's stopping and all the people are

   a. getting out.   c. sleeping.

   b. learning English.   d. buying clothes.

3. There's a big dog in the yard. He's eating his dinner. He eats fast. Now he has no more dinner. He's looking at us! Help! He's

   a. sleeping!   c. going away!

   b. coming here!   d. sitting down!

4. My friend has 15 cats. She has some gray cats and some brown cats. She has a beautiful, young white cat, but she has no

   a. brown cats.   c. brown dogs.

   b. little cats.   d. black cats.

5. Juan never drinks tea in the morning. He always drinks coffee. But he often drinks tea in the afternoon. He drinks tea and eats a cake

   a. at 12:00.   c. at 5:00.

   b. at 9:00.   d. for breakfast.

Exercise 2

➤ *Circle the best answer.*

1. Selma is from Istanbul. Now she lives in Toronto. She is a writer. She writes books for children. She is not rich, but she is happy. She likes her work, and she

   a. likes Istanbul.   c. doesn't like Istanbul.

   b. doesn't like Toronto.   d. likes Toronto.

(continued on next page)

2. Virginia lives in a very tall building. Her apartment is on the 40th floor. She likes to look out the windows. At night she can see

    a. cats and dogs.   c. the city lights.

    b. the sun.   d. a lot of children.

3. Leo has a very old car. It is 20 years old! It is not very beautiful, and it is not very fast. But it always

    a. goes.   c. comes.

    b. stops.   d. sees.

4. A big black cat lives in that house. It sits in the window all day. It likes to look at the people

    a. in the house.   c. on the street.

    b. on television.   d. in boats.

5. Tadek almost always has a sandwich for lunch. Sometimes he has an egg sandwich, and sometimes he has a meat sandwich. But today he doesn't want a sandwich for lunch. He wants

    a. some pizza.   c. a cheese sandwich.

    b. breakfast.   d. to eat at home.

Exercise 3

 Circle the best answer.

1. The Perez family likes to go to a Cuban restaurant. They go every Saturday evening. They meet their friends at the restaurant, and they have a good

    a. restaurant.   c. family.

    b. meal.   d. morning.

2. Dick likes to talk on the telephone. He often talks with his brother in Bombay. He sometimes talks with a friend in Berlin. And every Sunday he talks with his parents in Singapore. Dick pays a lot of money for

    a. clothes.   c. books.

    b. restaurants.   d. telephone calls.

3. Many people work all day. After work, they are tired, and they don't want to cook dinner. They like to eat dinner at

    a. home.   c. a shop.

    b. a restaurant.   d. work.

4. Susan and Sam don't eat French food very often. There is only one French restaurant in their town. The food there is not very

    a. old.   c. open.

    b. bad.   d. good.

5. For breakfast, Simon often eats eggs or meat. He always has bread and fruit. He drinks coffee or tea and juice, and sometimes he also has cake. Simon

    a. doesn't like to eat   c. doesn't eat any breakfast.
       a big breakfast.

    b. likes to eat a big   d. eats only a little breakfast.
      breakfast.

Exercise 4

➤ *Circle the best answer.*

1. Tina is in bed. The doctor says she is very sick. She must take some medicine. She can't get out of bed, and she can't go to

    a. television.   c. work.

    b. home.   d. children.

2. Donna's father is a doctor. Donna also wants to be a doctor. She wants to be a children's doctor. She likes children, and she wants to help

    a. them.   c. students.

    b. animals.   d. her.

3. Frank doesn't like to visit hospitals for children. He says they are sad places. In these hospitals there are many sick boys and

    a. doctors.   c. mothers.

    b. girls.   d. medicines.

4. You can't go to Tom's house today. He is very sick. The doctor is there now. He is looking at Tom, and he is asking Tom's mother a lot of

    a. money.   c. questions.

    b. medicine.   d. answers.

5. Dr. Kapoor gets up at 6:00 every day and goes to the hospital. In the afternoon, he goes to his office. He gets home at 8:00 in the evening. He has a very long

    a. work.   c. office.

    b. drive.   d. day.

Exercise 5

➤ *Circle the best answer.*

1. Many people have computers at work. Business people have computers in their offices. Teachers have computers at school, and doctors have computers in

   a. rooms.   c. hospitals.
   b. restaurants.   d. cars.

2. Harold works for a computer company. It is a big company. It has offices in many parts of the world. Harold often must go visit the offices

   a. in other companies.   c. before lunch.
   b. at home.   d. in other countries.

3. Many schools have computers. The children learn about computers in their classes, and the teachers use the computers for their

   a. lessons.   c. homework.
   b. schools.   d. offices.

4. Dan is an English teacher. He works for a big Japanese company. Some people in the company must speak English at work. Dan teaches them

   a. to understand in   c. about business.
      Japanese.
   b. Japanese.   d. business English.

5. There are three people in Mohammed's office. They all want to use the computer often, but there is only one computer! Mohammed says they must get another

   a. car   c. office.
   b. computer.   d. person.

Exercise 6

➤ *Circle the best answer.*

1. Surya is in another city for some business meetings. She must call her office every day. Her manager wants to talk with

   a. her.   c. them.
   b. him.   d. me.

2. The teachers at school often have meetings. They have meetings with the other teachers, and they have meetings with the

    a. school.   c. classes.

    b. company.   d. mothers and fathers.

3. Sandra doesn't like her job. She has meetings every week with her manager, and Sandra doesn't like

    a. business.   c. meetings.

    b. work.   d. mornings.

4. Chen has a new job in a store. He sees a lot of people. He must talk with them and help them, and he must

    a. never smile.   c. not open his mouth.

    b. smile a lot.   d. look at the floor.

5. Bus drivers are often very friendly. They sit in their bus for a long time. They like to talk to the people

    a. in their car.   c. on the telephone.

    b. on their bus.   d. in restaurants.

Exercise 7

 Circle the best answer.

1. These shoes are very beautiful, but they are also very expensive. I can't buy them now because I don't have much

    a. time.   c. money.

    b. color.   d. shoes.

2. Mara is getting a new pink dress. It's very pretty. Mara is very happy, but her mother is not very happy. The dress is very

    a. pretty.   c. old.

    b. expensive.   d. long.

3. We never go to the French restaurants in New York because they are expensive. We like to go to the Chinese restaurants or the Brazilian restaurants. They are not very

    a. expensive.   c. good.

    b. money.   d. big.

(continued on next page)

4. Tom and Shonni like to go to the Brazilian restaurant because there is often music. Sometimes a Brazilian group plays the music, and the people in the restaurant start dancing. Tom and Shonni

   a. like music and dancing.

   b. don't like music and dancing.

   c. like Chinese restaurants.

   d. like Brazilian shoes.

5. Pedro didn't want to get out of bed. He didn't want to have breakfast. He didn't want to go to work. He wanted to

   a. go home.

   b. take the bus.

   c. sleep some more.

   d. go to school.

Exercise 8

 Circle the best answer.

1. Anna is a student at the University of Texas. This is her first year. She is studying Spanish. She wants to be a

   a. French teacher.

   b. mother.

   c. doctor.

   d. Spanish teacher.

2. There are many students from other countries at Boston University. Some of these students know English very well, but the other students must

   a. study Chinese.

   b. learn to speak.

   c. study English.

   d. learn about Boston.

3. I like to go to this store because the people are very friendly. They always smile and say hello. They help you

   a. find things in the store.

   b. build a new house.

   c. get a new job.

   d. eat your meal.

4. Paula is the new manager of the company. At first, the workers didn't want a woman manager, but now they like her a lot. She's a very friendly person, and she always

   a. walks away.

   b. listens to them.

   c. looks at them.

   d. talks to women.

5. Suki didn't know any other students at first, but now she knows many of them. She says they are very friendly. They often meet in the cafe after class, and they always

    a. eat pizza.   c. ask her to come.

    b. ask other students.   d. go alone.

Exercise 9

> *Circle the best answer.*

1. Do you have any milk? There is a very hungry little cat here. It doesn't have a mother, and it wants something to

    a. love.   c. do.

    b. fish.   d. eat.

2. Jin often doesn't have time to eat lunch at work. She only has time for coffee. When she comes home, she is very hungry. She often

    a. doesn't eat.   c. opens some large boxes.

    b. eats some bread   d. has no breakfast.
       and butter.

3. Can you hear the baby? She's up in the bedroom, and she's crying now. I think she's hungry. Can you give her some milk? It's in the

    a. bottle.   c. place.

    b. dinner.   d. night.

4. Tommy cries every morning on the way to school because he doesn't want to go to school. He doesn't like the other children, and he doesn't like

    a. his mother.   c. his teacher.

    b. the street.   d. his breakfast.

5. Every night a cat comes into Sam's yard. It cries and cries, and it wakes up Sam. He gets angry and goes out to the yard. But he can never

    a. hear the cat.   c. change the cat.

    b. talk to the cat.   d. find the cat.

Exercise 10

 Circle the best answer.

1. Raissa's favorite color is blue. She has lots of blue clothes, a blue car, and a blue house. But she doesn't have blue eyes! Her eyes are

   a. big.   c. open.

   b. brown.   d. blue.

2. My parents' favorite restaurant is the Green Garden Restaurant. They like it because it has Chinese food. There is another good restaurant in town, but my mother and father don't go there. It doesn't have

   a. Mexican food.   c. Chinese food.

   b. any food.   d. good food.

3. Daryl doesn't eat lunch at school. She says the food is terrible. There are always hamburgers and pizza, and she doesn't like hamburgers or pizza. She likes to eat

   a. rice and vegetables.   c. terrible food.

   b. school lunches.   d. tea or coffee.

4. Shelley is a terrible student this year. She doesn't go to classes, she doesn't read the course books, and she doesn't do any homework. Her parents are going to be

   a. happy.   c. angry.

   b. hungry.   d. friendly.

5. We don't watch television very often. Our television is very old. We can't hear it very well, and sometimes we can't see it! The picture is in black and white, and it's

   a. beautiful.   c. new.

   b. very big.   d. terrible.

Exercise 11

Circle the best answer.

1. Bruce Wilson worked for the Acme Paper Company for 40 years. Then last year he stopped working. The people at the company were very sad when he stopped. Bruce was a good worker and

   a. a friendly person.   c. a terrible person.

   b. an angry person.   d. a young person.

2. There was a nice movie on television last night. It was the story of an Italian family. The men in the family had lots of problems. In the end, the men all went away. There were only women

    a. on television.   c. in the morning.

    b. in the family.   d. in Italian families.

3. Last year we had a very nice English teacher. She was friendly, and she was a good teacher. This year our English teacher is very different. She's often angry, and she's a

    a. new teacher.   c. tall teacher.

    b. first teacher.   d. terrible teacher.

4. What happened to Juanita yesterday? She wasn't in class. Trudy told me she had some family problems. Do you know about them? I called Juanita's home, but

    a. she was home.   c. there was no answer.

    b. Trudy doesn't know.   d. she has no phone.

5. Something terrible happened to my cat last week. She had a fight with another cat. She was away for three days. Then she came back, but she was

    a. very sick.   c. dead.

    b. not very young.   d. black and white.

Exercise 12

➤ *Circle the best answer.*

1. Something happened to the computer in the office yesterday morning. It stopped working, and we couldn't start it again. In the afternoon, we did all our work

    a. with the computer.   c. without the computer.

    b. out in the street.   d. on the blackboard.

2. We went to the hospital this morning. We wanted to see our teacher, but the doctor said no. He said she was still very sick, and he told us to come back

    a. yesterday.   c. to school.

    b. next week.   d. to the hospital.

(continued on next page)

3. John came to work late again today. He comes late almost every morning! What is the problem? Why is he often late? Doesn't he have a

    a. clock?   c. bedroom?

    b. bus?   d. desk?

4. Last year my friend Kiri went to Korea. She wanted to learn about the country and write some newspaper stories. But she had one big problem. She couldn't talk to people because she

    a. didn't want to travel.   c. couldn't speak English.

    b. couldn't speak Korean.   d. didn't have a newspaper.

5. Yesterday we went to see a funny movie. It was a story about love. A man named Jack loved a woman named Jill. Jill loved a man named Jarvis. Jarvis loved a woman named Janet, and Janet loved Jack. All these people had lots of problems, but the movie had

    a. an end.   c. bad color.

    b. a sad end.   d. a happy end.

Exercise 13

➤ *Circle the best answer.*

1. Many young girls like dancing and go to dance classes. They want to be dancers. They think dancers are beautiful, and they think dancing is fun. But a dancer's life is not always beautiful and fun. It can be very

    a. young.   c. pretty.

    b. easy.   d. difficult.

2. Help! There's a mouse in my room! It went under my chair, and then it ran under the bed. There it is again! It's running into the bathroom. Please come quickly and take it away. I don't

    a. like mice!   c. see any mice.

    b. eat any animals.   d. like any animals.

3. Today was a beautiful day. It wasn't very hot, and it wasn't very cold. There was lots of sun, and there wasn't any wind. It was a good day for

    a. working in the yard.   c. working in the office.

    b. sleeping.   d. looking at the television.

4. Last night we went to listen to some music. We didn't have a very nice evening. I almost went to sleep because the music was terrible and the room was

    a. nice.   c. green.

    b. friendly.   d. hot.

5. That child had many problems at school. The other children didn't like him, and the teachers were always angry with him. He told his parents, but they didn't

    a. see him.   c. teach him.

    b. listen to him.   d. wake him.

Exercise 14

➤ *Circle the best answer.*

1. How was your meeting? Was it interesting? Did you talk to the new manager? What did she say about your job? Are you going to stay at the same job, or are you going to

    a. sit down?   c. go to lunch?

    b. be late?   d. change jobs?

2. This morning I talked to Mr. Swenson. He told me some interesting news. The town wants to build a new road. They want to build it through his yard. He's very angry and upset. He doesn't want

    a. a road in his yard.   c. any roads in the town.

    b. a new town.   d. to build a road.

3. Yoko was very upset yesterday. Something terrible happened in Japan. There was an earthquake. Many buildings fell down in the earthquake, and about 5,000 people died. Many people now have no homes. They are living in

    a. houses.   c. Japan.

    b. schools.   d. families.

4. Mrs. Seurat was very upset because her son Bob never wanted to do his homework. He also never wanted to help her in the house. Bob was 16 years old. He wanted to lie in bed all day and

    a. learn English!   c. listen to music!

    b. work in the kitchen!   d. talk to his parents!

(continued on next page)

5. There was a dead cat on the road this morning. My daughter Leila saw the dead cat and started to cry. Poor Leila. She was very upset. She doesn't like to see

   a. dead animals.   c. lots of cats.

   b. lots of cars.   d. fast cars.

Exercise 15

➤ *Circle the best answer.*

1. Sven was the only child from Sweden. There were some children from Russia, Germany, and England. There were many Italian and Spanish children, but there were no other

   a. American children.   c. children.

   b. Danish children.   d. Swedish children.

2. Dicken started a new job last week. He likes the other workers, and he likes the work. There is only one problem. He doesn't like the manager. He says the manager is

   a. always nice.   c. always late.

   b. often angry.   d. often hungry.

3. Yussef is not doing very well at the university. He doesn't study for his English class. He only studies for his business class. He says English is not important and he doesn't want to

   a. find it.   c. learn it.

   b. feel it.   d. work it.

4. I have some big news for the family! We are going to move to another city next year. The children are going to go to a new school, and I'm going to start a new

   a. job.   c. car.

   b. day.   d. family.

5. My cat liked to sit on my car. It was her favorite place. She could see all the people on the street. She could also see all the dogs. The dogs could see her, but they couldn't

   a. hear her.   c. drive her.

   b. get her.   d. look at her.

Exercise 16

> *Circle the best answer.*

1. My brother didn't like playing football or tennis or other sports. He only liked bicycling with his friends. He often went out on his bicycle in the morning and came back in the afternoon. He and his friends went very fast. In a short time they could go

   a. a few miles.　　　c. home.

   b. another way.　　　d. many miles.

2. The bus to work is often very slow. There is a lot of traffic in the morning. Cars are slow, too, but bicycles are not. On a bicycle you can go around and through the traffic. Why don't you go to work by

   a. bicycle?　　　c. train?

   b. car?　　　d. bus?

3. Here's your sandwich and some fruit juice. Now take your bicycle and go! You don't want to be late for work. You were late yesterday and the day before. Go fast and

   a. stop often!　　　c. say hello!

   b. go home!　　　d. don't stop!

4. Look at all the traffic! We can't get off this road, and we can't go on that road. We have to sit here and wait. The radio doesn't work in this car, so we can't even

   a. get out of the car.　　c. go home today.

   b. listen to any music.　　d. read the newspaper.

5. Last March I was in Chicago for a business meeting. It's a beautiful city, and I liked it a lot. But I didn't like the weather! It was cold and very, very windy. Now I know why people call Chicago the

   a. "Windy City."　　　c. "Beautiful City."

   b. "Sunny City."　　　d. "Business City."

Exercise 17

➤ *Circle the best answer.*

1. Jorge's parents were very interesting people. His mother was a famous eye doctor. People came to see her from far away. His father had a famous Mexican restaurant. Many important people ate at his restaurant. One time, the American president

   a. had dinner there.
   b. was an interesting person.
   c. had breakfast in his room.
   d. went to a restaurant.

2. There was a letter on my desk. Now it's not there! Do you know where it is? It's a very important letter. It's from the bank. I must send it back soon, but I can't

   a. write it.
   b. learn it.
   c. give it.
   d. find it.

3. Lin lived in New York City. Sometimes she saw famous people near her home. Then she told all her friends at work. Her friends lived in New Jersey, and they didn't often see famous people. Not many famous people

   a. live in New Jersey.
   b. go to work.
   c. live in New York.
   d. have friends in New York.

4. Some people like to eat too many sweets. Their favorite foods are sweets. They eat lots of ice cream, cake, and cookies. They don't eat much fruit or vegetables. These people are often fat and unhealthy. Sometimes they get very sick. Sweets are not

   a. bad for people.
   b. good for people.
   c. new for people.
   d. expensive for people.

5. Look at that woman! All the people on the street are looking at her. She's very young and beautiful. She has very nice, expensive clothes. Now some people are taking pictures of her. I think she's famous.

   a. Who are they?
   b. What is it?
   c. Who is she?
   d. Where are we?

Exercise 18

➤ *Circle the best answer.*

1. Friday was the last day of the English course, and there was a party in the evening. The students bought some food and drinks. They got a stereo and some music. Then the party started. There wasn't enough food for all the students, but they weren't hungry. They wanted to listen to music and

   a. cook. c. study.

   b. dance. d. sleep.

2. Yesterday morning the bank was closed, so I couldn't get any money. I couldn't buy the newspaper, and I couldn't buy any milk or bread. I went to work with no breakfast, and I had nothing to read on the bus. At 11:00 I was very

   a. hungry. c. rich.

   b. full. d. tired.

3. There were many famous people at the party in New York City. There was the president of a big university and the president of a big company. There was a famous Swedish doctor and a famous Russian writer. There was also

   a. my friend Jane. c. a large party in New York.

   b. the wife of the French president. d. a lot of food.

4. Look at this place! Did you have a party last night? There are bottles and glasses on all the tables. There is food on the armchairs and on the floor. I'm going out for a few minutes. When I come back in a short time, I don't want to

   a. see this place! c. see these things!

   b. eat any food! d. have a party!

5. Sonya met a very interesting young man at the party last night. She told me all about this man. He's tall and good-looking. He has a very interesting job, and he likes to travel. He's not married, and he doesn't have a girlfriend. I think Sonya is

   a. talking on the telephone. c. married.

   b. in love with him. d. doesn't like him.

Exercise 19

> *Circle the best answer.*

1. Did you see the movie on television yesterday evening? It was the true story of a little Jewish boy. He lived in Holland in 1941. Then the Germans sent him and his parents to Germany. Jonah lived through this terrible time, but his parents died. It was a very good movie, but very

   a. terrible.   c. happy.

   b. wrong.   d. sad.

2. The English homework for tomorrow is very easy. We have to read one page of our book. We also have to do some exercises in the workbook. I can do it all tomorrow before class. I don't want to do homework this evening. I want to

   a. do my English   c. speak English.
   exercises.

   b. go out with my   d. do my Spanish
   friends.   homework.

3. The manager at work is angry with me. She says I am always late. She says I have to be in the office before 9:00 a.m. I can't come at 9:05, and she says I can't go home at 4:50. I can go home only after 5:00 p.m. She says I can't even go out for coffee! I have to drink my coffee

   a. in the office.   c. on the street.

   b. at home.   d. in a restaurant.

4. In 1994, Wanda opened a new store. She sold children's clothing. It was not easy at first, and she had many problems. But after a few years, business was good at the store. Many people in town bought clothes for their children

   a. from friends.   c. in big stores.

   b. at Benneton.   d. at Wanda's store.

5. Coffee was Ronald's favorite drink. He drank four or five cups of coffee a day. Then the doctor told him to stop drinking coffee. Ronald didn't know what to drink. He didn't want to drink tea. He said, "Only sick people

   a. drink coffee."   c. drink tea."

   b. drink milk."   d. go to the doctor."

Exercise 20

➤ *Circle the best answer.*

1. This is not a good place to live. The weather is terrible. In the summer, it's very hot here. It doesn't rain for three months. In the winter, it's very cold, and it rains all the time. There are only a few nice months
   - a. in the year.
   - b. for parties.
   - c. in Europe.
   - d. in the summer.

2. Do you have to go now? You can go home after dinner. I have a very nice meal ready for us. Do you like fish? I have fish and vegetables and rice. I also have cake and ice cream. Please don't go. I can't eat all this food! You must
   - a. go home now.
   - b. take the train.
   - c. help me.
   - d. not eat meat.

3. There was no train to our town, and there were only a few buses. In the morning, people drove their cars to work in the city. In the afternoon, people drove their cars home. On Saturday and Sunday, the city people drove out here to the country. There was always a lot of traffic
   - a. in the city.
   - b. in the winter.
   - c. on Mondays.
   - d. on our roads.

4. Rhonda doesn't like the winter in England. She doesn't like cold weather, and she doesn't like short days. She wants to live in a place with warm winters. She says she's going to sell her house and
   - a. build a new one.
   - b. start a business.
   - c. move to Morocco.
   - d. go live in Russia.

5. Last summer we went to the mountains for a month. We stayed in a beautiful place with lots of trees and flowers. The people were also very nice to us. The only problem was the weather. It rained every afternoon! This summer, we're going to go to the seaside. It doesn't
   - a. have many trees or flowers.
   - b. rain there very often.
   - c. have many people.
   - d. have any mountains.

Introduction
Vocabulary in *Basic Reading Power*, *pages viii–ix*

1. Draw a circle around the last word in this (sentence.)
2. There is a picture of a house below these sentences on the next page. Draw a circle around the house.
3. A word is missing from this *sentence*. Write in the word.
4. There are two blanks in the next *sentence*. Think of some words. Write them in the blanks.
5. My *mother* goes to *work* every day. (Other answers are possible.)
6. Draw a line from number 6 to number 1.
7. One word in this snetnece is not correct. Write that word correctly in the blank. *sentence*
8. ~~Cross~~ out the first word in this sentence. Then cross out the last word in this ~~sentence~~.
9. Draw a garden near the house below. Follow the steps in number 10.
10. Step 1. Draw a tree.
    Step 2. Draw some flowers.
    Step 3. Draw some grass.

Part One: Pleasure Reading
Introduction, *page 2*

1. a. no (Magda lives in Mosina, Poland.)
   b. yes (She takes the train to Poznan.)
   c. no (She doesn't always go home for dinner. Sometimes, she goes to a restaurant.)
   d. medicine (She wants to be a doctor.)

2. a. California
   b. no (He doesn't go home every weekend.)
   c. no (He can't speak Chinese yet. He is studying Chinese.)
   d. no (He wants to be a businessman in China.)

Part Two: Comprehension Skills
Unit 1: Scanning for Key Words

Exercises 1-8, pages 42–47
Answers may be checked by looking back at the key words in the exercises.

Unit 2: Scanning for Information

Exercise 1, page 48

A.
1. no	5. Natalie Merchant
2. August 17	6. 7:00 p.m.
3. Jethro Tull	7. $38, $28, and $23
4. four	8. May 26

B. Answers will vary.

Exercise 2, page 50

A.
1. two	6. $20 per hour
2. $350	7. 356-4678
3. one	8. June
4. yes (one)	9. $25
5. near University Road	10. Germany

B. Answers will vary.

Exercise 3, page 52

A. 1. .89 (89 cents)
  2. yes
  3. lemonade
  4. $3.79
  5. 28 ounces
  6. no
  7. Baby Juice
  8. eight
  9. two (Fruit Drinks and Baby Juice)
  10. four (4 ct. means 4 count)
B. Answers will vary.

Exercise 4, page 54

A. 1. 6
  2. units 1, 3, and 5
  3. Unit 4
  4. Ben & Jerry's Homemade, Inc.
  5. page 59
  6. units 2 and 5
  7. units 1 and 6
  8. Unit 4
B. Answers will vary.

Unit 3: Making Inferences

Note: With inferences, many answers can be right. If you can explain your answer, it could be right.

Exercise 1, page 57

1. in a clothing store
2. The man with the white shirt is a salesman. The young man is a customer. He is wearing jeans so maybe he is still a student.
3. The salesman is showing the suit to the customer.
4. The salesman is saying, "How about this nice suit?"

Exercise 2, page 58

1. in an airport, in the arrivals hall (Her bag has an airline baggage ticket on it.)
2. Many jobs are possible here.
3. They are shaking hands.
4. They are saying, "How do you do?" or "Nice to meet you."

Exercise 3, pages 58–59

1. coffee
2. meat
3. carrots
4. sugar
5. salt
6. bread
7. apples
8. rice or potatoes

Exercise 4, page 60

1. a school
2. a restaurant or a cafe
3. a park
4. a bank
5. a doghouse

Exercise 5, page 61

1. doctor
2. manager
3. president of a company
4. TV news reporter
5. bus driver

Exercise 6, page 62

1. near a river
2. He is hiding behind a big stone and calling for help. He is running from Bernie and Pete.
3. They are angry because Harry told them there was gold in the river. But there is no gold in the river.
4. Harry said there was gold in the river.

Exercise 7, pages 62–63

1. on a farm
2. He wants Sam to work.
3. because he is angry
4. Jenny thinks that because they don't have any money they aren't going to have any food.

Exercise 8, page 63

1. in a boat near an island
2. on the island
3. Yes, because he thinks it is a good place for pop concerts.
4. Duncan likes the island. He does not want pop concerts on it.

Unit 4: Looking for Topics

Exercise 1, pages 64-65

1. birds
2. hats
3. food

Exercise 2, page 66

1. color
2. music
3. animals
4. men
5. fruit
6. times of day
7. verbs
8. clothes
9. buildings
10. countries

Exercise 3, page 67

1. meals
2. women
3. reading material
4. drinks
5. jobs
6. furniture
7. transportation
8. tableware
9. sports
10. eating places

Exercise 4, page 68

1. computer
2. kitchen
3. bicycle

Exercise 5, page 69

1. family
2. garden
3. body
4. classroom
5. head
6. car
7. time
8. building
9. apartment
10. office

Exercise 6, page 70

1. People who work in government
2. People who often work at night
3. People who work in a hospital
4. People who make music
5. People who work with people
6. People who work with their hands
7. People who work with money
8. People who work outside

Exercise 7, page 71

1. Topic 1: fruit

   orange
   mango
   apple
   banana
   grapefruit

   Topic 2: sweet foods

   candy
   cake
   chocolate
   cookies
   ice cream

2. Topic 1: parts of a book

   chapter
   page
   table of contents
   paragraph
   title

   Topic 2: grammar words

   noun
   adverb
   adjective
   verb
   pronoun

3. There are many possible answers.

Exercise 8, page 72

Note: There may be more than one correct word for some topics. The topics are

1. park (garden)
2. head
3. food (things to eat)
4. transportation (ways to travel)
5. drinks (beverages)
6. men (relatives who are men)
7. times of day
8. reading material (things to read)
9. odd numbers (multiples of three)
10. body (parts of the body)

Exercise 9, page 73

1. head
2. rooms in an apartment or house. Extra word: wall
3. countries. Extra word: New York
4. sports you play with a ball. Extra word: hockey *or* Sports you play with many people. Extra word: tennis
5. verbs. Extra word: days
6. adjectives. Extra word: garden
7. car. Extra word: desk
8. time. Extra word: city
9. party. Extra word: read
10. cities (in the United States). Extra word: Canada

Exercise 10, page 74

1. drinks. Extra word: bread
2. transportation. Extra word: house
3. clothes. Extra word: clock
4. garden. Extra word: desk
5. women. Extra word: grandfather
6. body. Extra word: shoes
7. numbers by fives (multiples of five). Extra word: seventeen
8. Asian countries. Extra word: England
9. wild animals *or* zoo animals. Extra word: dogs
10. food. Extra word: spoon

Unit 5: Understanding and Building Sentences

Exercise 1, page 75

Note: You can also make other sentences. (But this way all the parts are used and no part is used two times.)

1. She's cooking fish.
2. She's drinking coffee.
3. He's reading a book.
4. He's sitting in a chair.
5. She's standing by the door.
6. He's driving a bus.

Answer Key

Exercise 2, page 76
Note: You can also make other sentences.
1. The dogs are eating their food.
2. The students are asking questions.
3. The children are building a doghouse.
4. My friends are buying new clothes.
5. Tom and Frank are closing the windows.
6. The girls are coming to play ball.
7. The women are getting their money.
8. The boys are helping their father.

Exercise 3, page 77
Note: You can use many different adjectives in each sentence.
1. The (young) man is driving the (green) car.
2. The (young) girl is eating a (big) sandwich.
3. A (black) cat sees a (brown) dog.
4. A (blue) bird lives in that (old) tree.
5. The (young) teacher is talking to a (bad) girl.
6. This (new) book is about (beautiful) cities.
7. (Small) children do not like (big) animals.
8. The (happy) woman is giving a (red) flower to a (handsome) man.

Exercise 4, page 78
Note: You can also make other sentences.
1. The horse is eating a (big) apple.
2. That house has (small) windows.
3. My sister doesn't like (long) dresses.
4. Simon's brother has (many) friends.
5. Some restaurants have (beautiful) flowers on the tables.
6. The students are talking to the (new) teacher.
7. The airplane is flying through a (white) cloud.
8. Mr. and Mrs. Jenkins cook (big) dinners on Saturday evenings.

Exercise 5, page 79
Note: You can also make other sentences.
1. I (often) read the newspaper in the morning.
2. I read English (slowly).
3. My family (never) goes to restaurants.
4. My father (usually) washes the windows.
5. I do my homework (quickly).
6. My friend rides a bicycle (badly).
7. I (usually) go to the bank on Saturday.
8. My mother drives a car (slowly).

Exercise 6, page 80
A. Note: You can also make other sentences.
1. A tall man is walking fast down the street.
2. That old dog always eats the cat's food.
3. Our morning class is learning to read well in English.
4. My baby sister wakes up often at night.
5. The new doctor is waiting for you.

B. There are many possible sentences.

Exercise 7, page 81
A. Note: You can also make other sentences.
1. Those girls often play baseball with the boys.
2. Some people don't eat meat.
3. My parents never have much free time.
4. Those men always eat very quickly.
5. Three children sometimes sleep in that small room.

B. There are many possible sentences.

Exercise 8, pages 81–82
1. a 2. b 3. a 4. a 5. b
6. b 7. a 8. b 9. b 10. b

Exercise 9, pages 82–83
1. Ho Kwangliang lives in Taichung, Taiwan.
2. He is the president of Ho Hung Ming Enterprises.
3. His company makes parts of shoes.
4. Many shoe companies buy parts of shoes from Ho's company.
5. Ho's company makes $25 million every year. or Every year Ho's company makes $25 million.
6. It has 100 workers in 8 buildings.
7. Now Ho has a new company in Shanghai, China. or Ho has a new company in Shanghai, China, now.
8. It makes parts of shoes, too.

Exercise 10, pages 84–85
1. his, They, their
2. he, his
3. it, he
4. it
5. They, their
6. She, her, it, her
7. She, them
8. their
9. She
10. He, his, his

Unit 6: Understanding Paragraphs

Exercise 1, pages 87–88

1. Yes. All the sentences are about one topic: Paul McCartney.
2. Yes. All the sentences are about one topic: Ringo Starr.
3. No. The sentences are about different topics.
4. Yes. All the sentences are about one topic: John Lennon.
5. Yes. All the sentences are about one topic: Brian Epstein.

Exercise 2, page 89

Asha Sachdev lives in Bombay, India. She is a very beautiful film star. Many people in India go to films. They all know and love her face. Other people see her face on the walls. There are big pictures of her face all around the city.

Exercise 3, page 89

Ho Kwangliang lives in Taichung, Taiwan. He is the president of Ho Hung Ming Enterprises. His company makes parts of shoes. Many shoe companies buy parts of shoes from Ho's company. Ho's company makes $25 million every year. It has 100 workers in 8 buildings. Now Ho has a new company in Shanghai, China. It makes parts of shoes, too.

Exercise 4, pages 90–91

1. b   2. c   3. a   4. c   5. c

Exercise 5, pages 92-93

1. a   2. c   3. c

Exercise 6, pages 94–95

1. Topic: The Irish writer Edna O'Brien
   Sentence: We can almost see the Irish countryside and hear the people speaking.
2. Topic: The Australian writer Thomas Keneally
   Sentence: He writes books about different places, so he has to go to those places.
3. Topic: The African-American writer Toni Morrison
   Sentence: We see through their eyes, and we learn what they are thinking and feeling.

Exercise 7, pages 96–97

Paragraph 1
Some kinds of drinks are very good for your health. Orange juice is one of these healthy drinks. It has lots of good things in it. Milk is another healthy drink. It is very good for children and also for women. So drink lots of orange juice and milk! Some doctors think this is the way to a healthy life.

Paragraph 2
Some popular drinks are not good for your health. Many people drink cola, but it is not good for you. It has lots of sugar, so it is bad for your teeth. It has other bad things in it, too. Another drink that can be bad for you is coffee. A little coffee is okay, but lots of coffee is bad. Doctors say it is bad for your stomach and your head.

Exercise 8, page 98

1. Topic: Rollerblading
   Extra Sentence: It is also a good idea to ride your bicycle.
2. Topic: How Jeff loves bicycling
   Extra sentence: He works just a few miles from home.
3. Topic: Tina's garden
   Extra sentence: Tina's husband likes going to the movies.
4. Topic: How Mike loves to cook
   Extra sentence: Children must not eat a lot of chocolate every day.

Part Three: Vocabulary Building

Unit 1: New Words from Your Reading

Note: Each student will learn different new words every week.

Unit 2: The 100 Words

Exercise 1, page 105

1. do	9. we	17. up
2. was	10. some	18. back
3. but	11. such	19. your
4. the	12. with	20. about
5. will	13. like	21. would
6. you	14. only	22. after
7. way	15. many	23. where
8. out	16. been	24. before

Exercise 2, page 105

1. so	9. even	17. could
2. more	10. said	18. which
3. been	11. even	19. years
4. all	12. down	20. their
5. were	13. time	21. next
6. them	14. over	22. these
7. yes	15. from	23. when
8. into	16. may	24. they

Exercise 3, page 106

1. your	9. here	17. would
2. what	10. any	18. them
3. have	11. this	19. our
4. new	12. time	20. about
5. said	13. two *or* the	21. she
6. then *or* than	14. what	22. well *or* were
7. that	15. even	23. other
8. can	16. most	24. down

Exercise 4, page 106

1. is
2. did
3. him
4. do, so, *or* to
5. here *or* were
6. time
7. when *or* then
8. many
9. may *or* way
10. but *or* out
11. now
12. by *or* my
13. which
14. their
15. other
16. where *or* there

Exercise 5, page 107

N A F T E R F R O M
E L Z O H A D B U T
W S R N I N A L L H
D O W N M A Y A R E
I M O S T N O C A N
D E V E N D U O F A
B E F O R E R X T N
L Z O U R S T H E Y
W L R P H A I M O O
A N E R E L N E B Y
Y T O M Y S O R C

Exercise 6, page 108

T H R O U G H L N O
I A B O U T O W O N
M S Y O U H V H W I
E V E N B E H E B Y
R N S I T S R R E T
B E F O R E Z E I F
A N Y F A B O U T I
C A N T W O U L D R
K N O O N A T H A S
M O S T O T H E R T

Some words found in this puzzle:
through, no, about, on, you, even, be, by, it, before, if, any, about, can, would, at, most, other, time, back, has, yes, these, over, out, where, now, first

Exercise 7, page 109

1. Allen: Would you like some milk with your coffee?
   Lynne: No, thanks. I like black coffee.

2. Suha: What is your name?
   Yuki: My name is Yuki.
   Suha: Is that a Japanese name?
   Yuki: Yes, it is.

3. Pat: Where are you from?
   Stan: I'm from Texas.
   Pat: Do you like to ride horses?
   Stan: No. Not all Texans like to ride horses.

4. Stefan: Do you like to read love stories?
   Milly: No I don't. I like to read about science and computers. They're much more interesting.

5. Craig: When did you call your mother?
   Ivan: I called her before lunch.
   Craig: Was she at home?
   Ivan: No, she was still at work.
   Craig: Where does she work?
   Ivan: At a bank in New York.
   Craig: Does she come back home for lunch?
   Ivan: No, she eats lunch at work.

Exercise 8, pages 110–111

Across:
1. my
4. would
6. We
7. back
9. next
10. are
11. not
12. They

Down:
2. you
3. did
5. like
6. When
8. after
10. about
13. be

Unit 3: Learning about Context

Exercise 1, pages 112–113
town, girl, yard, horse, meat

Exercise 2, page 113
sea, fisherman, boat, garden, evening

Exercise 3, page 114
daughter, housework, store, bread, friends

Exercise 4, pages 114–115
family, company, war, planes, countries

Exercise 5, page 115
Note: You can also put other words here.
books (stories), people, meat (food), weeks (months), children (girls)

Exercise 6, page 116
Note: You can also put other words here.
go, has (owns), run, drives, ends

Unit 4: Guessing Word Meanings

Exercise 1, pages 117–118
1. someone who doesn't like to work or do anything
2. a place where birds live and keep their babies
3. something you can wear so people can't see your face
4. something in a building that takes you from one floor to another floor
5. a person in a store who wants to buy something
6. a long line of cars in the road

Exercise 2, pages 118-119
1. fruit that is ready to eat
2. a bad dream
3. a poor person who asks for money on the street
4. things people don't want
5. something you wear on your hands on cold days
6. an animal that you have in your home.

Exercise 3, page 119
1. to pay to use something for a time
2. a kind of writing
3. some money that you get for a time and then pay back
4. to speak very loudly
5. a dirty place
6. a very large house

Exercise 4, page 120
1. a place to buy bread, cakes, cookies, or other baked foods
2. food that is very bad
3. something to put an animal in
4. a small road that is for people—in a park, the mountains, or the country
5. to make a person move
6. a girl who is good at schoolwork

Unit 5: Learning New Words in Categories

Exercises 1-8, pages 122–128
Note: There are many different answers to the exercises in this unit.

Exercise 2, pages 122–123
Some possible answers: artist, astronaut, bus driver, businessperson, movie star, musician, president, cook, teacher, policeman or policewoman, secretary, doctor

Exercise 3, pages 123–124
Some possible answers: keys, pen, money, lipstick, comb, Kleenex™, cellular phone

Part Four: Thinking Skills

Exercise 1, page 131
1. c   2. a   3. b   4. d   5. c

Exercise 2, pages 131–132
1. d   2. c   3. a   4. c   5. a

Exercise 3, pages 132–133
1. b   2. d   3. b   4. d   5. b

Exercise 4, page 133
1. c   2. a   3. b   4. c   5. d

Exercise 5, page 134
1. c   2. d   3. a   4. d   5. b

Exercise 6, pages 134–135
1. a   2. d   3. c   4. b   5. b

Exercise 7, pages 135–136
1. c   2. b   3. a   4. a   5. c

Exercise 8, pages 136–137
1. d   2. c   3. a   4. b   5. c

Exercise 9, page 137
1. d   2. b   3. a   4. c   5. d

Exercise 10, page 138
1. b   2. c   3. a   4. c   5. d

Exercise 11, pages 138–139
1. a   2. b   3. d   4. c   5. a

Exercise 12, pages 139–140
1. c   2. b   3. a   4. b   5. d

Exercise 13, pages 140–141
1. d   2. a   3. a   4. d   5. b

Exercise 14, pages 141–142
1. d   2. a   3. b   4. c   5. a

Exercise 15, page 142
1. d   2. b   3. c   4. a   5. b

Exercise 16, page 143
1. d   2. a   3. d   4. b   5. a

Exercise 17, page 144
1. a   2. d   3. a   4. b   5. c

Exercise 18, page 145
1. b   2. a   3. b   4. c   5. b

Exercise 19, page 146
1. d   2. b   3. a   4. d   5. c

Exercise 20, page 147
1. a   2. c   3. d   4. c   5. b

Teacher's Guide

Introduction

Basic Reading Power is intended for students who are in a beginning-level English program in junior high school, high school, college, or adult education. We assume that the students who use this book will be literate in their own language. They should have an English vocabulary of about three hundred words, and they should be familiar with the simple present, present continuous, and simple past tenses.

The aim of this book is to teach strategies that will allow students to build on their already established cognitive abilities and background knowledge. A strategic approach will enable students to view reading in English as a problem-solving activity rather than a translation exercise. This way, students can learn good reading habits and skills, and they can avoid problems that commonly result from poor reading habits. Students will gain confidence at this early stage, which, in turn, helps them to gain access more quickly to English-language material for study, work, or pleasure.

In *Basic Reading Power*, students are expected to work on all four parts of the book concurrently as they develop multiple aspects of their reading ability. This approach is essential for the successful outcome of a reading program using this book. *Basic Reading Power* is intended to prepare students for work in *Reading Power*, which has a similar general approach and layout.

General Guidelines for Teaching Reading with *Basic Reading Power*

- Actively engage students in the reading lesson. It is important for them to enjoy their work and not see the reading lessons as "busywork."

- Have students work in pairs or groups whenever possible. This helps them to develop new thinking styles and increases language acquisition.
- Focus on the thinking processes that the students use to complete the exercises. The right answers are not as important as how the students got those answers.
- Be sure that students know why they are doing an exercise. Awareness of the purpose of their work helps the students become involved more actively and results in increased learning.

Part One: Pleasure Reading

The goal of this part of the book is to introduce students to the idea of extensive reading and to give them the opportunity to experience the rewards of such reading in terms of both improved reading ability and general language ability. To participate successfully in extensive reading, they will need to gain confidence in their abilities and to experience the satisfaction and enjoyment that such reading can bring. For these reasons, teachers should allow students maximum freedom in pacing their reading, choosing their books, and expressing their opinions. Two other factors are also essential for students to discover the pleasure in pleasure reading: a relaxed and trusting atmosphere in the classroom and a high level of enthusiasm and commitment on the part of the teacher.

The extent to which students benefit from their pleasure reading, however, depends on how they go about it. Thus, in this part of the book, students are introduced to some of the ways native speakers approach such reading.

These ways include the following:

- reading for the meaning of a story
- predicting what comes next in a story
- responding to the ideas in a story
- relating parts of a story to their own lives
- skipping over unknown words
- breaking a story into parts (analysis)
- talking about a story

The pleasure reading material in the book consists of an introduction, ten fables, ten short stories, and one long story. It is important that students read these fables and stories in the order presented because the vocabulary and grammatical structures in each story build upon those in previous stories. In the last section of Part One: Pleasure Reading, students are encouraged to read books for pleasure, and they are guided in the selection of appropriate books.

As mentioned above, the first ten readings are fables. Since fables are a part of every culture, students will find them easy to relate to. The next 11 stories are about people. They are not fables. You should point out to the students that many of the stories are true or could be true. These stories also provide material for discussion of cultural differences. The main goal for the teacher throughout is to guide the students in learning how to respond to these fables and stories.

Guidelines for Reading the Fables and Stories

General approach

- Encourage students to talk about each story before, during, and after reading it. As they talk, the students make important connections: They connect what they already know and can express in their own language with what they read in the story.
- Lead the discussion at first, in order to model the process for the students. If necessary, provide and practice specific vocabulary for the students to use in such discussions. When the students have had sufficient practice, they should be allowed to lead the discussion themselves.
- Use the first fable ("The Big Family in the Little House") as an example with the class. Go through all the reading steps together with them.

Before reading a story

- Encourage the students to preview the story. Tell them to look at the title and at any illustrations accompanying the story and to identify what they see.
- Lead the students to make predictions about the story by asking them the following questions. Be sure to have them explain their answers as well.

  What is the story about?
  Who are the people in the story?
  Where are they?
  Is this story about today or about the past?
  Do you think it is a sad story or a happy one?
  Do you think the story is true?

- Ask the students to read the first paragraph of the story. Then have them make more predictions about what comes next.

Reading the story

- Ask the students to read the story silently all the way through. Tell them not to stop for new words or to mark the text in any way while they are reading. This would distract their attention from the story itself.
- Do *not* let students use dictionaries while they are reading! Tell them they will have an opportunity to deal with the new words later on.
- Put the students in small groups and ask them to retell the story to each other. Then you can reconstruct the story together as a whole class.

After reading the story

- Discuss with the students their responses to the story by asking them the following questions:

  Did you like this story? Why?
  Who is in the story?
  Do you think it is a true story?
  How did the story make you feel?
  Is the ending a good one?
  How could we change the ending?

- Ask students to read the story again. If an illustration accompanies the story, tell them to label parts of it with names and words from the story.

- Ask students to look back at the story and underline any new vocabulary. They should write those words on the lines below the story or in a notebook and look up the meaning in their dictionaries. They may need help in finding the correct meaning and in wording a satisfactory definition. Model the process and assist students in acquiring independence in the use of dictionaries.

Additional activity

As a whole-class activity after reading the story, ask students to brainstorm about other possible endings. Working with the whole class, ask the students to dictate the best ending they have come up with. Write that ending on the board and then ask students to copy it into their notebooks. More confident students can be asked to do this activity in small groups. After some practice, individual students can try to write their own endings and then compare their endings with those of other students. Have students write another ending as a homework assignment.

Pleasure Reading Books

Evaluating students' progress

There are a number of ways you can evaluate students' progress and comprehension in their pleasure reading books. Whatever method you choose, however, you must keep the "pleasure" in mind. Therefore, feedback to students should be positive and should focus on their personal reactions to their reading. In addition, students' output, whether oral or written, should not be judged on pronunciation or grammar.

Here are some ways to evaluate pleasure reading:

- **Individual teacher/student conferences.** This is the best way for you to come to a quick assessment of each student's understanding of what he or she is reading. These conferences can give the student an opportunity for a one-to-one discussion with you in which you can model ways that native speakers talk about literature. The focus of these talks should be the student's response to the book, rather than a retelling of the story. By giving individual attention to students, these conferences can also help students build confidence in their abilities.

Avoid asking individual students to stand up and report on their reading orally in front of the whole class, which could be damaging to the students' self-confidence.

- **Pleasure Reading Book List.** (See text, page 38.) Keep track of the number of books read by referring to this list. As a variation, keep book lists for each student posted in the classroom. With younger or competitive students, this tactic can act as a spur to motivation, though care must be taken to keep the competitive aspect from becoming too serious.
- **Writing about pleasure reading books.** (See text, pages 38–39) This letter-writing activity encourages students to put down on paper their thoughts about a book in an informal context. The letters can be written in class or assigned as homework. Then students can exchange letters, or you can select some letters to read aloud or write on the board. Other students who have read the same book can be asked their opinions. The emphasis of any discussion should, as always, be on the students' reactions, not on details of the story.
- **Pleasure Reading Report.** (See text, page 40.) Though long, formal book reports are not recommended, a short report following this format could be filled in by the student on completion of each book and kept on file in the class or in the student's notebook. They can then be read aloud and compared if more than one student has read a particular book. In addition, if they are kept on file in the classroom, students can refer to them in choosing books.

Choosing books for pleasure reading

The limited vocabulary of the students does not necessarily mean a limited choice of reading material for them. Many publishing companies produce books for the beginning, or "starter," ESL/EFL level, with a wide range of subject matter to interest both younger and more mature students.

Many teachers have found that the question of how to provide pleasure reading for all their students can best be resolved by the institution of a class lending library with a few more titles than there are students so that each student will be able to choose a book. It may also be possible to combine libraries with another teacher or teachers or to set up the pleasure reading collection in the school library. In this case, however, students need to have free and frequent access to the library.

Aside from being able to choose subject matter that is interesting to them, students also need to be free to choose books at an appropriate level. Be sure to include books at a somewhat higher level for those students who quickly gain confidence and want more challenging reading as well as very easy books for those students who progress more slowly.

Listed here are a few of the many available titles from the most widely distributed publishers.

Very Low Level

Addison Wesley Longman

Longman Easystarts—200-word vocabulary. These books are all 16 pages long and come with a cassette recording of the text. Examples:

April in Moscow	Stephen Rabley
Between Two Worlds	Stephen Rabley
Dead Man's River	Elizabeth Laird
Dino's Day in London	Stephen Rabley
Who Wants to Be a Star?	Margaret Iggulden

Longman Originals—Stage 1: 300-word vocabulary. Cassettes available. Examples:

Ali and His Camera	Raymond Pizante
Marcel and the Shakespeare Letters	Stephen Rabley
Mike's Lucky Day	Leslie Dunkling
The Missing Coins	John Escott
The Wrong Man	Kris Anderson

Longman Structural Readers—Stage 1: 300-word vocabulary. Cassettes available. Examples:

Aladdin and His Magic Lamp	A. Stempleski
Car Thieves	L. G. Alexander
The Flying Spy	Alwyn Cox
Green Island	A. G. Eyre
Kate and the Clock	Leslie Dunkling
The Mystery of the Loch Ness Monster	Leslie Dunkling

Heinemann Educational Books, Inc.

Heinemann ESL Guided Readers—Starter Level: 300-word vocabulary. Examples:

Alissa	*The Lost Ship*
Blue Fins	*Sara Says No!*
The Briefcase	*Ski Race*
L.A. Detective	

More Advanced Level

Oxford University Press

Oxford Bookworms—Level 1: 400-word vocabulary. Examples:

The Coldest Place on Earth	*The President's Murderer*
The Elephant Man	*Under the Moon*
Love or Money	*White Death*

Addison Wesley Longman

Longman Structural Readers—Stage 2: 500-word vocabulary. Examples:

Adventure Story	*and Other Short Stories*
The Boy and the Donkey	
Girl Against the Jungle	
Have You Got Our Ticket?	
Shakespeare Detective	

Longman Classics—Stage 1: 500-word vocabulary. Examples:

Alice in Wonderland	Lewis Carroll
Black Beauty	Anna Sewell
Heidi	Johanna Spyri
The Three Musketeers	Alexandre Dumas

Longman Originals—Stage 2: 600-word vocabulary. Cassettes available. Examples:

Another World	Elaine O'Reilly
Fire in the Forest	Ian Swindale
Wanted: Anna Marker	Kris Anderson

Heinemann Educational Books, Inc.

Heinemann ESL Guided Readers—Beginner Level: 600-word vocabulary. Examples:

Dangerous Journey	*This Is San Francisco*
Death of a Soldier	*This Is New York*
The Long Tunnel	*The Truth Machine*
Rich Man, Poor Man	*The Wall*

Part Two: Comprehension Skills

General Guidelines

- You should always make sure that the students understand the purpose of the exercises they are doing and how the particular skill relates to general reading ability. Otherwise, the exercises become busywork and the students lose interest.
- The whole class should work together when the teacher introduces and works on the first exercise in a unit.
- Model the thinking processes that students need to use to carry out the exercise. That is, you should "think out loud" in front of the class so that students can learn about those processes and the language used to talk about them.
- Have the students work in pairs or small groups whenever possible.
- Since the exercises in each unit become gradually more difficult, students should always work on them in the order in which they are presented.
- The exercises in this part of the text should be approached as much as possible in a spirit of playful competition. When the exercises are treated like games and the atmosphere of the class is relaxed, students become more involved and feel freer to take risks.
- For some of the exercises, students may give answers that are different from those in the Answer Key, and any reasonable answers should be accepted as long as the student can justify them.

Unit 1: Scanning for Key Words

The scanning exercises in units 1 and 2 are designed to help students get over the habit of reading every word on a page. In scanning, students must quickly look for specific information, skipping over unneeded words. In this unit, students scan across a line for a key word. Note that the words used in the exercises are from the list of the "100 Words" in Part Three, Unit 2. In doing these exercises, students will also be working to improve their sight recognition of these important words— the 100 most common words in English. (You can refer to page 163 in this Teacher's Guide for more information about the 100 words.)

Since speed is essential to the aim of scanning, encourage students to work quickly, either by timing them or by conducting the exercises as a kind of race among pairs of students.

Unit 2: Scanning for Information

In these exercises, students scan a variety of real-life materials for the answers to some specific questions. In doing this, they will learn to move their eyes quickly across a page and not be distracted from their search for information. Again, speed is important. The material in this unit can also serve as a source for discussion of certain aspects of U.S. culture and how they compare with other cultures.

Note that students should not use a dictionary while working on the scanning exercises, but should skip any words they do not know. Discuss some of the vocabulary afterwards in a general discussion about the material.

Unit 3: Making Inferences

In English, students will often have to "read between the lines" in order to get the meaning of a passage. To do this, students must be willing to make guesses—which means taking risks. These exercises will help them gain confidence in their ability to infer meaning in a reading text.

In this unit, getting the "right answer" is less important than the thinking process that students go through to get their answers. Allow students the opportunity to come up with different answers if they can justify their ideas based on information in the passage.

Unit 4: Looking for Topics

In English text, ideas are generally expressed and developed in a "topic-centered" way; that is, writers first give the topic and then they comment on it. In learning to read in English, it is essential that students begin early on to think in terms of the topic.

These exercises work best if the students work in pairs. That way, the two students can help each other when one or the other does not understand. Furthermore, in talking to each other about the topic, the students will develop their metacognitive ability to think and speak about text in terms that will help them to comprehend what they read.

Unit 5: Understanding and Building Sentences

Students at this low level need practice forming good sentences and identifying the parts of the sentences most important to the meaning. Though this is not always thought of as a reading skill, it is important to remember that the thinking processes involved in reading and writing are often inseparable. The ability to find meaning in a sentence is a skill that good readers in English frequently take for granted.

In these exercises, students will have the opportunity to be creative in forming sentences. However, the sentences must always be grammatically correct and reflect correct usage. Note that in exercises 1, 2, 4, 6, and 7, there are several possible ways to connect the parts of the sentences but only a few ways that they can be connected into correct sentences using each part only once.

Unit 6: Understanding Paragraphs

This unit aims to provide the students with practice in recognizing the topic-centered nature of English texts. Students must first understand that good comprehension depends on the reader's ability to identify the topic. Good readers, in fact, are always unconsciously or consciously looking for the topic as they read.

Students then need to understand how a paragraph in a text focuses on a topic. For that reason, the purpose of the first three exercises is to familiarize students with the difference between a paragraph and a random group of sentences. Students who need more practice in recognizing the form of a paragraph can be given this further assignment: Tell students to choose one of the groups of sentences about the Beatles that makes a good paragraph (1, 3, or 4) and write the sentences in the form of a paragraph. Point out that they should begin the paragraph by indenting the first sentence.

As they write out the sentences in paragraph form, the students will have an opportunity to notice again that every sentence in the paragraph refers to the same topic. Often beginning-level students need this kind of reinforcement in order to internalize both the form and the topic-centered nature of a paragraph in English.

Exercises 4 through 8 give the students practice first in recognizing the topic and then in thinking of the topic and stating it in comprehensible form. Where students are asked to think of the topic, various answers are of course acceptable, as long as they express the topic correctly (neither too specific nor too general).

In this unit, as in all the other skills units, allow time for discussion about how the students came up with their answers. Encourage students to talk explicitly about the thinking processes involved.

Teachers who are looking for further work on topics of paragraphs will find a more extensive treatment (at a high-beginner level) in *Reading Power*.

Part Three: Vocabulary Building

Research in second-language reading confirms what many teachers know by instinct and experience: Building vocabulary is an essential factor in reading improvement, especially at the lower levels.

In this part of the book, students are encouraged to build vocabulary in various ways. All the exercises, however, present unfamiliar words in meaningful contexts so that students can learn to use such contexts to figure out meaning through the application of cognitive skills. In fact, the more cognitive capacity required in the process of figuring out meaning, the more likely students are to fix the word and the meaning in their long-term memory.

For this reason, students should be discouraged from using their dictionaries or asking friends or teachers for the meanings. Instead, encourage them to try to establish meaning first by thinking about the context and making guesses. Only then should the dictionary come into play, as a means to check the guesses. This approach is established from the very beginning, in Part One of the book, where students are asked not to use dictionaries while reading for pleasure.

Unit 1: New Words from Your Reading

This unit should be introduced after students have read several of the fables in Part One: Pleasure Reading. Below each fable, students will have written some new words. They should then choose ten of these words to transcribe onto the pages of this unit.

These words may, of course, be different for different students, thus allowing them to develop their own personal vocabulary learning project. Having learned the procedure for writing the new word, the sentence or sentences, and the meaning, students should then continue this practice in their own notebooks. Ideally, these should be small notebooks that they can easily carry around and that are used exclusively for this purpose.

At the end of a week or other given period of time, have students test their knowledge of the new words of that week by giving themselves a New Words Quiz (see page 103). Verify that students quiz themselves in this way at regular intervals throughout the course.

Unit 2: The 100 Words

In this unit, students are asked to focus their attention on the 100 most common words in English. Although these words are often taken for granted by teachers, they are not always easily learned through context, and they often constitute a serious stumbling block for the beginning reader. Be aware, in fact, that these 100 most common words make up 50 percent of the words in an English text of average difficulty! If students have to stop and think about these words, their reading speed and comprehension will obviously suffer.

Therefore, it is essential that students learn to recognize these common words on sight. That is the aim of this unit and the reason students are asked to concentrate on the spelling and form of each word, rather than the grammar or meaning.

Unit 3: Learning about Context

In this unit, the students are introduced to the concept of context in vocabulary learning. Emphasize the relationship of the word to the general context of the story or the more specific context of the sentence, and ask students to be explicit about the reasons for their choice of words. In exercises 1 through 4, the missing words are given to the students, but in the later exercises, students are to think of the missing words. They may come up with some different answers from those suggested in

the Answer Key; these should be accepted as long as they make sense.

Unit 4: Guessing Word Meanings

In this unit, students are now faced with words that are probably unfamiliar to them. In order to arrive at some kind of meaning for the words, they must tap their own experience and knowledge of the world. Note that students should ideally try to write definitions in English, however vague or circuitous they may be, as this is excellent practice. However, if that is not possible due to the level of proficiency or maturity of the class, they may write equivalent words in their own language.

You should go through the first exercise with the whole class as a group, and model the thought processes that help the reader use the contextual clues to arrive at a hypothetical meaning. Afterwards, have students try to do several items on their own and then work in pairs to compare their answers or figure out together meanings they haven't deciphered individually. If you are working with students whose language is unfamiliar to you, students should do this pair work with another student who speaks the same language, especially if students cannot think of the word in English but can think of an equivalent word in their own language.

Unit 5: Learning New Words in Categories

This unit builds on the use of students' own life experiences to help them learn new words in categories. Grouping the words in categories puts them into context for the students and so increases the probability of retention. Furthermore, the personal involvement required in the exercises is a further positive influence on the acquisition and retention of the vocabulary. Therefore, these exercises require a large degree of individual input on the part of the students and allow them to choose the vocabulary to be learned to a large extent.

For the first exercise, after making sure that the students understand the example in the text, do another example as a group. For this second example, focus on *your* favorite place, providing some vocabulary and soliciting other words from the class. The other exercises can be approached in a similar manner, with less guidance as students become more confident.

In exercises 4, 6, 7, and 8, encourage students to create categories that reflect their own life experience, and after each exercise ask them to explain their categories to the class. For example, in exercise 4, one student might put "mountains" in "Village Life" (e.g., a Swiss village) and another student might put "mountains" under "City Life" (e.g., Mexico City).

Part Four: Thinking Skills

These exercises provide practice in some of the basic thought patterns of English. Students can solve the problems presented in the exercises by applying such patterns as synonymy, opposites, analogies, negation, part-whole relationships, and drawing conclusions based on evidence.

The exercises gradually become more difficult, so it is important that they be assigned in the order they are presented in the book. Once again, the use of dictionaries should be discouraged while students work on the thinking skills exercises.

In this part of the book, students should work alone. Once all the students have completed a set of problems, either in class time or as a homework assignment, check them together in a group session in which students volunteer to read the items aloud. Encourage students to express their disagreement if they have different answers and ask them to explain how they arrived at those answers. This kind of discussion can help them externalize their thinking processes and lead them to greater metacognitive awareness.